STRENGTHENED BY STRUGGLE

Also by Michael Baughen

Breaking the Prayer Barrier
The Moses Principle

Strengthened by Struggle

The Stress Factor in 2 Corinthians

Michael Baughen

Harold Shaw Publishers
Wheaton, Illinois

Cover photo: Gary Irving

ISBN 0-87788-792-6

Library of Congress Cataloging in Publication Data

Baughen, Michael A.
      Strengthened by struggle.

      1. Bible.   N. T.   Corinthians, 2nd —Criticism, interpretation, etc.
I. Title.
BS2675.2.B347   1984   227'.307   84-5496
ISBN 0-87788-792-6

Printed in the United States of America

93 92 91 90 89 88 87 86 85 84   5 4 3 2 1

To my three families:
my human family: my wife Myrtle, and
*   Rachel, Philip, and Andrew;*

the church family of All Souls, Langham Place,
*   London, where I have ministered as Rector, and*
*   where 2 Corinthians burned into my soul;*

the wider family of the Diocese of Chester, in whose life
*   I now share as Bishop.*

With thankfulness to God for all the love and
*   encouragement experienced in all three families,*

and with particular thanks to Roger Barley, Helen
*   Hartley, and Pippa Dobson for their willing help*
*   in typing the manuscript for this book.*

CONTENTS

CHAPTER 1

INTRODUCTION —THE HOT LETTER

MOST PEOPLE FACE the prospect of letter-writing either with reluctance or with eagerness. If it is a thank-you letter for a birthday present we may struggle for words, but if it is a love letter we can often go on and on—and on!—as our tender thoughts flow onto paper. Yet probably the most passionate of letters will be written when we are deeply concerned for those who are in serious trouble, or going astray in their lives, or compromising the Christian faith. Then our writing will burn with the fire of loving concern. Second Corinthians is that sort of letter—the most passionate and earnest of Paul's letters, the hottest letter of the New Testament.

The Corinthian church was active and, on the surface, successful. The people demonstrated love and zeal, and took part in lively worship. But Paul sees beyond the surface to the reality beneath and he is deeply concerned about what he discerns.

Perhaps success had gone to the Corinthians' heads,

encouraged by false teachers who had infiltrated the church. These teachers were certainly not regarded as false teachers by the Corinthians, but Paul could see their real motives. In order for them to successfully distract the Corinthians from the truth, the false teachers first had to denigrate the previous teachers and instructors. In spite of all Paul had done for them, the Corinthians were easily turned against him by these new teachers.

Their line of argument was that if Paul were a true apostle he ought to be living a triumphant, trouble-free life. They argued, it seems, that Christians should be free of all suffering and illness, that the Christian life should be at a level above the norm. They argued that Paul obviously was not living at that level; consequently, he was unworthy of the title of apostle and was not the sort of person to listen to or follow. These new teachers professed to have something better to offer—a higher level of Christian living, a super-spirituality that suited the Corinthians' pride.

The false teachers had also lulled the Corinthians into an inactive faith. They had encouraged such a spiritual complacency—an inward-looking Christianity that was concerned only with its own joy, pleasure, excitement, and satisfaction—that evangelism had taken a back seat. Paul is deeply concerned, and powerfully argues for the urgency of evangelism (chapters 5—6). He knew, as we realize today, that any church that is concerned only with itself to the exclusion of outreach and concern for the world will die. This attitude also made the Corinthian church careless toward other churches, lacking concern for the urgent material need of sister churches. Two whole chapters of this letter (8 and 9) form the most powerful and persuasive argument for real Christian giving in the whole Bible.

Once the church starts emphasizing feelings and experiences more than facts, it has begun to walk a dangerous road. The Corinthians were proud of the special, even spectacular, spiritual experiences in their congregation. Yet, as 1 Corinthians 15 indicates, they began to lose their concern for accuracy in doctrine. Some, perhaps, taught that as long as Christians had the right sort of experience, what they believed did not matter much. Perhaps they argued that Paul was too cerebral; they had found experience-centered Christianity to be much more satisfying. 1 Corinthians 15 makes clear that they had grown careless about the truth of Christ's resurrection and, like many today, were saying that as long as the Christian individually experienced the resurrection life, the fact of Christ's literal resurrection mattered little. Paul forcefully refutes that idea in 1 Corinthians 15, and in this second letter (especially chapters 10—13) he continues to express his deep concern that the Corinthians should be clear on the fundamentals of the Christian gospel.

In balance with issues of doctrinal truth, Paul emphasizes moral living that accords with the Word of God. The readiness of the Corinthian church to allow moral error into their assembly was alarming to Paul, and has been an alarming feature of experience-centered Christianity ever since.

Churches that are cerebral and cold, without the warmth of real fellowship and sharing in the grace of Christ, need spiritual fire. Churches that are experientially warm but have ceased to value expository preaching and in-depth teaching need spiritual correction. This urgent, ardent letter of Paul can awaken the former and correct the latter. It is a letter of outstanding relevance to the church of our day.

Greetings:

Grace and Peace (1:1). Before Paul plunges into the issues of the letter, he offers greetings which teach us several important concepts. First, we should observe that Paul writes with authority. He designates himself as an apostle, whereas Timothy is called "our brother," and the members of the church in Achaia are "saints." Although the title "apostle" was sometimes used in the more general sense of "someone sent," its primary significance in the New Testament is as a reference to the Twelve and Paul.

The apostles were all personally commissioned by Christ, and Paul had himself received a dramatic call on the road to Damascus. They were set apart by God by the signs done through them (Acts 2:43), just as Jesus had been shown to be who he was by "signs" (John 2:11). The church, then, was "built upon the foundation of the apostles and prophets, Christ Jesus himself being the cornerstone" (Eph. 2:20); the successor to that apostolic authority is the New Testament, where the apostolic doctrine is preserved.

The popular idea that we can have apostles today with similar authority to Paul's is a grievous misunderstanding of the authority of the New Testament. The subsequent teaching that such present-day "apostles" have authority equal to the teaching of New Testament apostles is heresy. What we handle here in 2 Corinthians is from the hand of one who was designated an apostle by Jesus Christ and so has the authority of God. 1 Corinthians is not merely an interesting piece of writing, but the Word of God, for us to hear and obey.

The letter is addressed especially to the church at Corinth. "Church" here means, of course, the believers in the city of Corinth. They are not just a random collection of individuals, but part of a cohesive group, a family, a body. Christianity is not an individual matter that we sometimes share in with other individuals—it is baptism into the body of Christ, and carries with it the mutual responsibility of love, care, encouragement, and learning. Even the word "saints," which Paul applies to all the Christians in Achaia, is a corporate word, used sixty-three times in the New Testament, always in the plural (except for one instance where it is singular but the meaning is plural—Phil. 4:21). The Christian cannot be an individual "saint." He or she is part of God's family, and "one of the saints"—one of those belonging to the Lord. Christianity cannot therefore be only an individual experience any more than a person can live in a human family and have nothing to do with its other members. Like Paul, we must be concerned not only with our own Christian lives but also with the life and witness of the church of God—both locally and worldwide. We are part of it; we rejoice with it and weep over it; we pray for it and work in it.

The grace and peace Paul extends to his readers applies to us as well. He wishes us to experience that grace in all its love, mercy, forgiveness, direction, and kindness; the overflowing grace into which we have been brought and by which we are to grow and serve. And he wishes us to have peace in the middle of every storm, every pressure, and every challenge, the peace which passes understanding and which comes from God alone.

Questions for Study and Discussion

1. Although the Corinthian Church was growing and active, what problems threatened to undermine Paul's work there? In what ways does the twentieth century church manifest some of the same problems that were present in Corinth?

2. What constitutes a correct balance between the "cerebral" and the "experiential" aspects of the Christian faith? How can we as Christians work to achieve that balance?

3. Paul attacked the false apostles who were leading the Corinthians away from the truth. What kinds of false teachers are present in the church today? What kind of enticing doctrines do they present that might seduce people from the true faith?

4. Why was Paul's apostleship a key issue in his authority among the Corinthians? How can we as Christians respond positively to God-ordained authority?

CHAPTER 2

PRESSURE AND PRAISE

1:2—2:13; 7:2—15

SUFFERING: PAUL KNOWS more about it than all the false teachers put together; he knows it to be no discredit to his apostleship but rather an evidence of his true following of Christ. And he does not waste a moment getting into that burning theme.

Jesus Christ was called "the suffering servant" in Isaiah's prophecy (Isa. 53). He did not tell his disciples that following him would be a picnic in the sunshine, but that it meant denying themselves and taking up the cross. We, too, are called to drink the cup of suffering as he did. The early disciples experienced cruel persecution, suffering, and death by torture—torn to shreds by lions in the arena, and even crucified. Suffering has been inherent in Christian testimony since Christ's crucifixion; it still is today, across all the continents of the world.

Samuel Rutherford put it like this: "God has called you

to Christ's side, and the wind is now in Christ's face in this land; and seeing you are with Him you cannot expect the lee-side or the sunny side of the brae." Yet some evangelists and Christian testimonies lead us to expect only sunshine, or milk and honey!

Living under pressure

The key word in this first chapter is "troubles" (NIV) or "affliction" (RSV); the Greek word is *thlipsis*, in verses 4, 6, and 8. It means "pressure"—physical pressure from a heavy weight on our body, but also mental or spiritual pressure—certainly an apt word to describe modern humanity. We all seem to live under pressures:

The pressure to "conform"—Romans 12:1—2. The world wants us to conform, says Paul, using a word meaning "pressure from without" like the pressure from the jelly mold that shapes liquid Jello. The world is irritated by "nonconformists," Christians who stand up for Christ's standards. It wants to squeeze each of us into its mold. The pressure on us all from the media and from the opinion of our peers is enormous.

The pressure of life itself—illness, sorrow, bereavement, unemployment, starvation, poverty, disappointments, frustrations, wars, broken relationships, hopes and dreams unfulfilled. We experience such pressures whether we are Christians or not, simply because we live in a fallen world.

The pressure of a world without Christ—the overwhelming size of the evangelistic task, the spiritual blindness of our friends and relations, the wealth and power of the Arab States in promoting Islam, the despair of untouched millions, the worship of materialism, the moral chaos. All this spells agony for the world.

The pressure of false teaching. Not only do we have to contend with atheism and apathy but with false teaching and active heresy—cults that ensnare people, making them prisoners of error.

The pressure of attacks upon us for our faith—persecution, mockery, sarcasm, and rejection by our unsaved friends.

What a relevant word *thlipsis* is! And if we can add to the list from our own experiences, just think how much more Jesus must have felt this pressure! He saw sin clearly and experienced our fallen world from the viewpoint of the One who had created it in its perfection. In all this, but particularly when we suffer for our faith, "the sufferings of Christ flow over into our lives" (1:5, NIV).

God's comfort

We naturally groan about suffering. It is never pleasant, and all of us would like to be free from it. The false teachers at Corinth taught that Christians ought to be free from suffering, to live above such experiences; the flaw in such teaching, however, is that it leads believers to want heaven now. We will only be truly free from pressure and suffering when we leave our earthly bodies and go home to the Lord.

Some teach that we should praise God for suffering, thus gaining the victory, but that is a way of deception and despair. Paul, in contrast, praises God (v. 3), because he knows that whatever pressure comes upon him, whatever suffering he has to endure, the comfort of God sustains him. God's comfort under pressure really *is* something to praise about! And Paul's genuine testimony is enhanced by the testimony of millions of other believers.

What is the comfort offered by God? The word is *paraklesis,* sharing the same root as *paraklete*—the word Jesus uses for the Holy Spirit in John 13—16 ("Comforter" in the KJV and "Counselor" in RSV). *Para* means "alongside" and *"klesis"* means "called." Comfort, then, is God coming alongside. It is not necessarily a lessening of the pressure or trouble, though it may include such relief, but rather it is the added gracious presence of the Lord. The psalmist in Psalm 23 reflects this comfort vividly. When he is by the still waters he talks about "The Lord ..." but when he passes through the valley of the shadow of death he says *"You* are with me." The close personal relationship with the Lord intensifies in the experience of trial as demonstrated by the testimony of Christians through the ages. "The Lord was so close to me ... I was marvelously supported by the Lord ... I have come to know the Lord more closely and intimately through this experience." When we think of the most wonderful Christians we have met, we usually think of those who have endured suffering, yet glow with the faith and love of Jesus.

I was fascinated as I flew across the desert between the Grand Canyon and Las Vegas to see pools of water dotting this otherwise parched landscape. Psalm 84 came to mind: "As they pass through the valley of Baca (suffering) they make it a place of springs—the autumn rains also cover it with pools." Similarly, Christians who have gone through a desert experience in life and drunk deeply of the wells of God's comfort and grace make their wilderness a place of refreshment.

Certainly there is no stinginess about the comfort God gives as he comes alongside; Paul testifies (v. 5) that "as the sufferings of Christ flow over into our lives, so also through Christ our comfort overflows." Not just in small quantity, nor even a larger one carefully measured out, but free, full, and running over!

Comfort is for sharing

A British railway enthusiast like me knows the difference between a Euston experience and a Crewe experience.

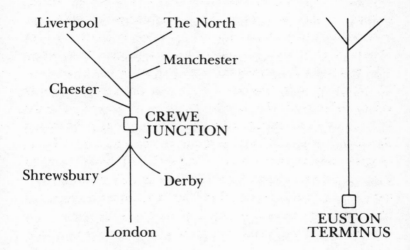

Euston is a terminus. All trains stop there and can go no further. It is the end of the line and the final destination of all trains.

Crewe is a junction. Some trains terminate there, but most of them go on. You can change at Crewe. Going north, the lines branch off to Liverpool, or to Preston and Scotland, or to Manchester, or to Chester and North Wales. Going south you can branch to Shrewsbury, or to Derby, or to London.

Paul says, in effect, that comfort is to be a Crewe and not a Euston. It is (v. 4) "so that we can comfort those in any trouble" or (v. 6) "if we are distressed, it is for your comfort and salvation; if we are comforted, it is for your comfort."

It is natural to want comfort in Euston terms, to desire it only for ourselves. We are going through this experience and we are the terminus and destination of all the comfort God brings. But Paul insists that we see that although we are part of the destination, we are also to be comfort junctions, sharing and passing on to others the comfort that has come to us.

Christians are likely to experience more suffering than non-Christians, rather than less suffering, because of the value it brings in comfort ministry. An old Arab proverb declares: "All sunshine makes a desert"; it is not easy to share comfort with others unless we have had illness or suffering of our own.

Learning to comfort

Comfort is more easily given, of course, if the affliction someone else is experiencing is identical with what we have been through ourselves—if we can say "I had miscarriages too" or "I know what mental illness is like" or "We know what it means to lose a child in an accident." But in this we are not confined to what we have suffered. The principles and experience of comfort help us comfort others "in any trouble," and we are to bring to bear "the comfort we ourselves have received from God" (v. 4). This puts on us the responsibility of learning through God's comfort and observing what has really helped us.

We may be devastated by the death of a husband or wife, and the aching void is never filled. At the same time, as we draw on God's comfort, we should prepare to help others going through the same valley later. Sometimes God's comfort is very practical; the cake and water was more important for the spiritually-depressed Elijah than a sermon or a text. Sometimes the quiet presence of a friend in Christ means more than talking. As we learn from the way God comforts us, directly and through others, we can become more effective ministers of Christ's comfort to others.

Troubles can increase our faith

In verses 8—11 we see Paul getting even more blessing out of affliction. The experience itself he describes vividly as being so unbearable that they believed they were going to die. J. B. Phillips translates it: "We told ourselves that this was the end." The word he uses is the one used to describe a ship sinking under a load or of people breaking under strain. We might describe it as "the bottom dropping out."

Some years ago I was a leader at a boys' camp in Surrey, supervising active youngsters aged ten to thirteen. We went down to Littlehampton for the day and there by the sea was a large amusement park with bumper cars, a big dipper, and much more. Up came one of the boys. "Come on the rotor, sir?" I did not know what a rotor was, but I could not think of a way of saying "No" to the boy without looking like a coward! So I yielded.

"Here, sir," he said, and led me through a door into a very large cylinder. People were looking over the top with disconcerting grins on their faces! "Just stand against the wall, sir." I did. "It'll go round in a minute, sir." It did. And as its circular motion speeded up and I was spread-eagle against the wall, wishing I had never said "Yes," he added with an impish grin, "They'll take the floor away in a minute, sir!" They did! I remained pinned to the wall by the force of the rotor. That was (almost!) Paul's experience here. The floor had dropped away, and he despaired of life itself.

Does Paul argue with God? Does he complain or moan at God? Does he ask, "Why has this happened to me?" No! Instead, with the certainty born of closeness to God, he sees that such an experience has a purpose (v. 9): "that we might not rely on ourselves but on God, who raises the dead." In a tidal wave of troubles that would cause many Christians to give up, Paul threw himself upon God. No one else could deliver him. Rather than losing faith in such a moment, he had faith to the uttermost.

Help! Start praying!
Paul looks back upon that time in Asia and, thankful that God delivered him then, goes on learning and applying God's promises. Now he is going through a similar experience, but he does not start from square one. He carries with him what he learned last time. He sets his hope (v. 10) on deliverance this time, too, and he encourages the Corinthians, who were more inclined to criticize, to help and share with their prayers. Paul can see a further blessing—if many people pray, many people will share in the praise and thanksgiving when God answers.

In our churches, the prayer gathering should be the generator of the church. There we share challenges and needs in prayer, and there we go on giving thanks and praise as God answers prayer in different ways. Often I have shared tears of joy with fellow Christians after God has brought us through a great venture of faith or has met with someone in the congregation in a special way. Recently I visited a church where, on the previous Sunday, the church family had wept in prayer for a child who had been injured in an accident and was on the verge of death; God had wonderfully met the needs of the child, and on this Sunday they were overwhelmed with praise and thanksgiving.

Sometimes we have to be brought to the point of help-lessness to realize how our faith is diluted by dependence on our skills, our talents, or the support of the fellowship. One man I ministered to struggled for weeks with the decision to make a commitment to Christian faith. He was afraid to come to Christ because of the cost to himself and his businesses. He could see that Christ was Savior and Lord; but he could also see that a commitment would mean becoming honest, and—ultimately—finan-cial ruin. After getting in his car one night and driving "aimlessly" for hours, he came back and yielded to Christ in my rectory at midnight. The honesty that resulted ruined him—almost. The police arrived on his doorstep to evict his family and take possession of his belongings, but then God worked a miracle. He and his wife rebuilt their lives with Christ, and the lesson they learned in those overwhelming circumstances has produced growth ever since in their committed lives. They have learned and relearned that such experiences of overwhelming affliction are "to make us rely not on ourselves, but on God who raises the dead."

Who'd want to be a leader? (1:12—2:11; 7:2—15)

Sometimes affliction comes to us from fellow Christians. When we are in positions of Christian leadership we are often the targets of unloving action, bitter criticism, hurt-ful misrepresentation, and wounding misunderstanding. I sometimes wonder whether some people feel they can fire their guns at a Christian leader because they do not think he or she should fire back!

Paul does not fire back, but he does not let them go on in their misunderstanding, either—he takes time to ex-plain and plead from the heart. As he says in 2:5, this kind of pain affects everybody. It is not just the person attacking or being attacked; others are caught up in the conflict, and the pain of one member affects the whole body. Healing, therefore, must also come to the whole body.

We must love, even if we fail in everything else (1:15—2:1). The Corinthians had accused Paul of vacillation. He had said he would come to them on his way to Macedonia and he had not done so. Could his "yes" and "no" be trusted? Paul's "yes" and "no" were utterly reliable, for he stood on the promises of God, was commissioned to serve God and was, like the Corinthians, sealed by the Holy Spirit. He did not say one thing and mean another. Rather, they had miscontrued the facts of the story. Paul had indeed changed his plans, but not deceitfully or carelessly—he had done so out of true love for them. A visit from him would have caused them pain, and he wanted to spare them. Instead of coming, he had decided to write a letter to them—and this was difficult enough for him. He wrote (2:4) out of "great distress' *(thlipsis)* and anguish of heart and with many tears. His love for them was overflowing.

Soon after I was first ordained I had to go to a home to explain a disciplinary action taken against the family's teen-age son. Afterwards the mother remarked about my words, "If only he had said it with love." It was a fair rebuke. It is easier to discipline without love, but we must not do so. In the years of my ministry since then I have had to use discipline in several complex situations. I have normally been able to share that action with my church elders or other close counselors or fellow ministers. Discipline is always immensely costly; the pain has often kept me awake at night as I have wondered what to do and how to do it. The hurt to the church family, when the situation has been known, has sometimes been deep. Yet the deepest concern is that we act with a balance of discipline and love.

Christ's body must restore the fallen member in deep love. After discipline, restoration must begin (2:6—11). Restoration is not possible without genuine sorrow and penitence, but clearly the person concerned here (v. 7) has shown deep sorrow for his act. Back in 1 Corinthians 5:5 the man had been "delivered to Satan for the destruction of the flesh that his spirit may be saved." Now, he needed to be drawn back into the fellowship with true forgiveness so that Satan would not bring into the church a spirit of hardness and lack of love. Paul is alert to the devices of Satan; elsewhere (Eph. 4:26—27) he warns that letting the sun go down on our wrath gives opportunity to the devil. We need to be careful in discerning the heart and mind of Christ in such complex and sensitive situations in the church. In Corinth, the painful incident was dealt with by direct action, love, and involvement. To have evaded the issue and not acted would have left a festering sore to poison the whole body. Action had to be taken— but in deepest love.

The Christian leader feels the most pain. The church leader who is, humanly speaking, ultimately responsible for discipline feels the agony the most deeply. There is no other human being to whom he can "pass the buck." He may get advice and share with others; he will pray and wait on the Lord; but in the end he must carry the matter on his heart. In verses 12 and 13 of chapter 2, Paul tells us that even though he had an open door for the gospel, he could not rest. He longed to know what had happened, how the church had reacted, and he had no telephones or telegrams to speed the news! So he went to

Macedonia to find Titus who had been sent to Corinth.

Chapter 7:2—16 provides the sequel. Even in Macedonia Paul had no rest, but "conflicts on the outside; fears within"—like the "fightings without and fears within" from the hymn "Just as I am"—until Titus came with encouraging news. The Corinthians had shown a godly grief and had been eager to rectify the circumstances. So Paul is full of joy, comfort, and peace, and his heart goes out to them: "You have such a place in our hearts that we would live or die with you." Once again, in different circumstances, he can testify (7:4) that in the middle of difficulties he is filled with comfort; his "joy knows no bounds." No wonder he could begin the letter (1:3—4) with the testimony from the depths of his heart: "Praise be to the God and Father of our Lord Jesus Christ, the Father of compassion and the God of all comfort, who comforts us in all our troubles, so that we can comfort those in any trouble, with the comfort we ourselves have received from God."

Questions for Study and Discussion

1. What are some common misunderstandings among Christians as to the causes of suffering? Read 1 Peter 2:19—25; 4:12—19. How do these verses show that suffering can be a credit to a Christian's life and a testimony of God's goodness?

2. What kinds of comfort does God give to those who suffer? How does our own suffering prepare us to give the same kind of comfort to others around us?

3. Paul demonstrated honesty with the Corinthians even when that honesty meant severe rebuke. Why is such correction necessary for continued growth? How is reproof a demonstration of deep love and commitment?

4. Hebrews 12:1—15 describes God's discipline of his children. What positive results come from discipline? What negative effects can come from resistance to discipline?

CHAPTER 3

SERVANTS OF THE LORD

2:12—4:6

As HUMAN BEINGS, we have no greater privilege than to serve the Lord, although from the way some Christians act, you would think Christian service was a nuisance! We must never lose our sense of awe and wonder at the fact that God, our God, the God of the universe and eternity, is relying on us. When we are helping others in his name, or speaking, or working in a camp, or inviting someone to a Bible study, or using our talents in other ways, we should see it as a holy privilege. This whole letter throbs with the heart of a man on fire with love for Christ and totally committed to use his life in the Lord's service. He does not splash around in the shallows but strikes out into deeper water. He does not offer God the leftovers of his time and energy but gives his best.

Paul is also deeply conscious that he does not serve alone. He is a worker with God, cooperating with the Holy Spirit and ministering a gospel that comes to life in people's hearts and lives by the Spirit. He is aware of his responsibility to handle God's truth faithfully and not casually, for the Holy Spirit will not honor the mishandling of the truth.

Where should you serve him?

Christians always seem to be interested in guidance and how to know God's will. Several times a week I talk to individuals about God's guidance in their lives. A young man in his first job may feel ill at ease, sure that he is in the wrong job. Another senses a call to the mission field —is it of God or not? Another asks for advice about a personal relationship. The questions multiply; people really do want to know God's will for their lives. If we are not asking such questions, something is wrong with our commitment.

Guidance, however, is seldom a direct word from the Lord, but a matter of balancing inward conviction with outward circumstances, surrounding everything with heartfelt prayer and a real submission to God. 2 Corinthians 2:12—13 gives one glimpse of guidance. Paul finds an open door to preach the gospel in Troas but does not stay because he has no inward peace. When we find an open door for ministry it may not always be right to step through it, for we find doors open in countless directions. The need and opportunity to preach or serve in one town is matched by the need in ten thousand other towns. Thus Paul said good-bye to the people in Troas and set off for Macedonia. If he had been at peace in his heart, presumably he would have stayed in Troas until either the circumstances changed or the inward peace departed from him.

Christians should not flit about like butterflies, merely

to enjoy different spheres of action for Christ. Sometimes God calls us to stay in the same place and in the same task for him throughout our entire lives. To move would be to step outside the will of God. However, in 2:12 Paul's outward circumstances and inward peace did not match up. He had great concern about the Corinthians, and he had no way of finding out what was happening. Titus, the one person who could tell Paul the situation, was not there at Troas. The absence of Titus at that moment was itself a segment in the pattern of guidance. Until the Corinthian situation was sorted out Paul could not be at peace. A simple "casting all our care on the Lord" would not rectify this situation; it needed healing action. Fellowship had been broken. Until it was repaired, Paul could have no real peace in service. In a similar way Jesus tells us in his Sermon on the Mount that if we are offering a gift at the altar and there remember that our brother has something against us, that we should first go and be reconciled to our brother before offering the gift (Matt. 5:23).

Remember you are on the King's side! (2:14)

In spite of having to leave Troas and its "open door" Paul did not mope around with a look of failure on his face. He was always in Christ's triumphal procession. Whether he was on the boat crossing to Macedonia, or waiting at the quayside, or spending the night at a hostelry (the predecessor of the motel) he was still Christ's man.

We are all tempted to live in compartments, with the Christian side dominant at suitable times but neatly packed away when it becomes inconvenient. There are many who entirely separate their "business life" from their "Christian life," but it is an impossible separation in God's eyes. We are his servants *always* and should be manifesting our Christian faith in every section of our lives.

In 1975-76 when we rebuilt All Souls, Langham Place in London, the architect was a fine Christian as well as a brilliant architect. He insisted that every site meeting begin in prayer. The tough builders, engineers, and sub-contractors soon got used to it, and as time went on they began to see that God was significantly answering prayer in the details of the building. They knew that the church members were praying with expectancy and determination. The brief prayer at those site meetings made them see, and later testify, that this was more than just a job— all because the architect was unafraid to bring his living Christian faith into the business arena.

The King has triumphed

We, too, are part of a "triumphal procession" (2:14). Such processions were frequent in the world of Paul's day, where the Romans loved the pomp of such events. The really great processions were reserved for the returning conquerors, and none were so magnificent as those in Rome: Crowds of people, in a mood for celebration, line the long straight road, talking about the great victories won by the army and about the skill of the commander. The commander, honored above all, rides on his chariot at the center of the procession, his immediate family with him or near him. The army marches upright and proudly, enjoying the celebration of their commander's victory. But the conquered are also shown off to the crowd, walking with drooping shoulders, defeated and captive, heading for death or slavery.

Paul puts Christ at the center of this picture. What

greater victor is there than Christ? What greater triumph is there to celebrate than his? At the name of Jesus every knee will bow and everyone will acknowledge him to be the Lord—whichever part of the procession they find themselves in. The victory was won upon the cross, and the triumphal procession has already begun. Paul sees himself (and we must see ourselves) as part of it, so that whatever he does for Christ is done in the context of that victory procession. Even his diversion from Troas to Macedonia is still in that procession of triumph. Like Paul, every Christian is part of the family of Christ, and so we also walk in the joy of his triumph.

But there are others in that procession, as Colossians 2:15 describes them: "Having disarmed the powers and authorities, he made a public spectacle of them, triumphing over them by the cross." When we rejoice in the triumph of Christ—and we had better rejoice—we declare the conquest over Satan and the legions of evil, and we declare that there is a greater power than theirs. The King has triumphed—forever!

You have an aroma!

Advertisers make sure we are conscious of "body odor" or of "bad breath," persuading us to use perfume and after-shave, each with a special aroma or fragrance. We are not unaccustomed to the spreading of fragrance.

Paul's image in 2:14 is not of after-shave, but the smell of the incense that filled the air as it was disseminated by the priests. Yet Paul applies the picture personally. Those who are "in Christ" are involved in spreading the fragrance of the knowledge of Christ. Just as people become conscious of a woman wearing perfume or of a man with strong after-shave, so others are to become conscious of the fragrance of Christ when they meet us. We are to have about us that "unmistakable something" —the aroma of Christ, the fragrance of his love. Great eloquence or martyrdom (1 Corinthians 13 reminds us) is useless without love. Christians who want to serve the Lord must have lives that breathe out Christ, or else their words are empty.

The essence of this fragrance is "the knowledge of Christ," not articulation of information but a demonstration of the personal fellowship with Christ in our lives. For many people there is a big jump from an "arm's-length" knowledge of Christ to a personal knowledge of him.

A few years ago I was at a conference of ministers and lay-readers, a large conference accompanied by observers and reporters from different church traditions. At the final dinner of the conference a reporter from a church newspaper said, "What I cannot get away from is the fact that everyone here seems to know Christ personally." The fragrance of the knowledge of Christ had spread through many lives. Many may disagree with what we say, oppose what we say, and even mock what we say, but they cannot deny the genuineness of a Christ-centered life.

Recently I received a number of letters from a mother about her daughter, who has come to Christ and has become a lovely Christian, caring, serving, and radiating Christ. Because of incidents earlier in life when the parents caused harm to the daughter, the mother cannot accept that her daughter does not condemn them. She is angry that the daughter is so loving and kind! This girl's life spreads the fragrance of the knowledge of Christ.

The aroma has contrasting effects

The incense diffused in the Roman General's procession had contrasting meanings: to the soldiers and the conqueror's family it signified victory; to the captives it signified defeat and death. The results are similar in Christ. The aroma of Christ spread by Christians reaches two sorts of people (2:15): "Those who are being saved and those who are perishing." The effects are that the first smell the aroma as a fragrance of life; the others as a fragrance of death.

The fragrance of life draws Christians together wherever they meet. In almost any part of the world we can find fellow-believers and experience an immediate oneness in Christ that minimizes differences of language, color, or culture. When we meet others on a bus or a plane and find they are also Christian, an immediate rapport is established. We are part of a worldwide fellowship of those who are, like us, "in Christ," and we are drawn together by that fragrance.

Yet at the same time, the person rejecting Christ finds the aroma of Christ an irritant. He does not like it; he resents it and is often angered by it, because it acts as a convicting fragrance. Deep down he has tried to bury any faith he might have had, and Christians remind him of it by their lives.

A student, for example, may come to living faith at the university and then go home on vacation to godless parents. Their reaction is predictably one of horror and antagonism. They do not rejoice in the transformed life, the improved morals, and the new values; they only react. They are being convicted by the fragrance of Christ in the life of their son or daughter. Hence, the persecution or antagonism can often be sharpest from those who once had some spiritual awareness but have rejected Christ. While being prepared for such hostility, we should also welcome it as a sign of the convicting work of the Spirit in that person's life.

The Lord smells the aroma

In the Old Testament (Gen. 8:21) we have the picture of Noah's sacrifice after the flood, a "sweet-smelling savor" to God. Similarly, in verse 15, Paul speaks of our being to God the aroma of Christ. Our spreading the fragrance of Christ brings delight to the Father; he loves to see Jesus being uplifted and honored. We bring joy to him when our lives are effective in encouraging other believers or convicting unbelievers. Influencing others is possible for every Christian, not just the preacher or the evangelist or the leader. Wherever we live, whatever we do; whether in a quiet secluded sphere or in a position of authority, we are to spread the fragrance of Christ by the way we live— and the Father will be delighted.

Who is equal to such a task?

Paul's question in verse 16 is a good one to ask. A group of students, all preparing for ordination, traveled to a tough city area in the north of England. They were to spend a day visiting house to house in that area. As the bus passed through the outskirts of the city, the tension grew. Suddenly, a student at the front of the bus, hands rustling rapidly through the pages of his New Testament, called out, "Where is that text: 'Who is equal to such a task?'?" We all empathized with his cry! Which of us can possibly be equal to any task for Christ; particularly, in the context of this verse, the task of spreading the fragrance of Christ by our lives in the office, the hospital, the university, the shop, the home, the neigh-

borhood? Paul gives the answer in 3:5: "Our competence
(NIV)/sufficiency (RSV) comes from God." In my own
strength I cannot be equal to the task of spreading the
aroma of Christ; it is only possible if I am daily refilled by
his Holy Spirit and as the Holy Spirit transforms me
gradually towards the measure of the stature of the fullness of Christ.

Spread the word

Once people are aware of the knowledge of Christ in our
lives, we must match that by a faithful sharing of the
word of God and by showing others the light of the
gospel. We may spend a long time explaining the gospel
to a friend only to hear them say, "Yes, I must try
harder!" We may feel we have failed, but perhaps our
work has not been matched by the work of the Spirit. We
need to surround each such conversation with prayer,
training ourselves to use half of the mind to speak and
converse, the other half to pray. Witnessing is a partnership task between the ministry of the word and the ministry of the Holy Spirit; however accurate we may be in
preaching the word, it is useless unless the Spirit brings
light.

Don't be a peddler (2:17)

Paul offers a strong warning about how *not* to handle the
word of God—"not, like so many, peddlers of God's
word." The peddler was a hawker, a street salesman,
often a swindler. We may admire his skill and wit, his
ability to persuade customers that junk is valuable, his
techniques in selling "rubbish," simply by clever tongues.
But all the eloquence in the world will not increase the
value of their products.

The church has always been plagued with peddlers of

the word. Like the market peddlers, they are supremely confident that their brand of Christianity, their divergent emphasis, or their special super-spirituality is the only way. Such "super-spiritual" people lose discernment and fall into heresy. Anything labeled with their brand of thinking is regarded as acceptable; anything not so branded is unacceptable. They like quick results—the peddler wants an immediate purchase before he moves on.

One mark of peddlers, according to Plato, is that they praise all their stock whether it is good or bad for the purchaser. The Christian "peddler," too, is often concerned primarily with "scalps"—pressuring people into decisions, and leaving others to sort out the damage. Patient sowing and nurturing can be destroyed in an evening by forced evangelism or false "healing" or "deliverance."

The peddler is often dishonest and manipulative with his goods; he uses sleight of hand and a slippery tongue. The Christian "peddler," often an effective speaker or writer, may also manipulate the word. People believe he must be right because "he puts it over so well." The false apostles plaguing the Corinthian church were such peddlers, leaving the church in confusion and division.

We condemn such peddlers of the word, but do *we* also peddle the word? Are *we* guilty of manipulation or selectivity that does not take account of the whole truth of God? Paul reaffirms his stand in 4:2, "We have renounced secret and shameful ways; we do not use deception, nor do we distort the word of God."

Speak with God's authority (2:17)
Instead of peddling the word, Paul declares, "We speak before God with sincerity, like men sent from God." We

may begin by sharing the word of God with others, perhaps in a small study group. We may even proclaim the word and speak in meetings. We are conscious of our friends, our minister, our non-Christian hearers. Only gradually do we begin to be conscious of God and our responsibility to him, realizing that we are handling his word in his sight. Such awareness makes preaching an ever-increasing privilege and an ever-increasing burden —a burden of the responsibility of handling God's word to others.

Paul could describe himself as called by God to this task, as an apostle; ministers, too, have a special call in the church. Yet the task is for the whole church. When we declare the word, we should not do it apologetically, nor weakly, but "like men sent from God."

Authority which manipulates the word of God is dangerous, but authority sincerely submitted to the word is dynamic. We easily impose our own ideas on the word and think it is saying what we want it to say. But when we submit to the word, work at it, meditate until we thoroughly grasp what God is saying, then we can deliver it in confidence, with his authority.

When I was first ordained I found myself cornered by the opinions of people rather than by the word of God itself. An accepted standard of interpretation was expected and anyone who stepped outside those boundaries was written off as "liberal." I was invited to join a group of young ministers who met to discuss the word together. Submission to scripture was the only rule. My first meeting was liberating! Accepted ideas were discussed and challenged on the basis of what the Bible taught. One notable minister, a leader in the church, made a statement which was challenged, to my amazement, by a much younger minister. The older man looked at the Bible passage being quoted by the younger man and then humbly said: "You are right, my brother." I was amazed—and thrilled. Here at last I was seeing a sincerity about the word of God! It brought a release to my whole ministry and to my spiritual life.

God's letter writing

Our job is to be mail carriers for Christ. A letter from Christ is to be delivered (3:3), a letter written by the Holy Spirit and written on human hearts. We cannot do the writing, but we are involved in the delivery. We speak the word: the gospel of Jesus, his free offer to every person. The Spirit makes that word alive in the hearer.

How wonderful when we open the Word of God to someone and they see and believe! The miracle of spiritual rebirth always inspires wonder at God's work in that person's life, in response to faith. The Holy Spirit has brought them into Christ; the letter from Christ has truly been written on their hearts.

When the Corinthians wanted "letters of recommendation" (3:1—3), Paul responds: "Look at these converts and their growth in the Spirit—they are my best recommendation." Some Christians may belittle others or question their commitment because they do not have a certain mark or have not "spiritually arrived" in a particular area, yet God continues to work in the lives of many people in those churches. That is God's recommendation, and it is the only one that matters!

This passage teaches us the limits of our task. We are commissioned to speak not with our own competence but with the competence of God and his new covenant. We are not to water down, adapt, or replace this word of

God. The methods of delivery may alter, but what we deliver remains the same.

The moment of faith and rebirth ushers the believer into eternal life—a new life that will endure, that does not fade away. Chapter 3 verses 7—11 compares the glory of the old covenant through Moses with this new covenant through Christ. This new one will never fade— it lasts forever. When we help someone into real faith in Jesus we see the beginning of a new life forever—a moment, therefore, of colossal significance and results!

Target for change

The Spirit not only brings us to eternal life but begins an immediate work of transformation. The world thinks that becoming a Christian means entering into law-keeping, but the Spirit shows that it is the beginning of true freedom, freedom from the world's conformity, freedom for a new relationship with the Lord (4:17—18).

The partnership between the word and the Spirit continues. On our side we are to "contemplate" (NIV margin) the Lord's glory. The word means "gazing into" as into a mirror, and thus can be translated "reflect" as in the main text of NIV. The more we contemplate the Lord's glory—who he is, what he did for us on the cross, and all he has shown us of himself in his word—the more we shall find the Spirit transforming us. The transforming is not automatic, nor does it take place without our co-operative contemplating. Gradually over the years, as we know more of him through sermons, Bible exposition, study, and meditation, the Spirit changes us into the likeness of Christ, the goal of every believer.

Becoming like Jesus Christ is the most important and

wonderful transformation that can happen to a human being, and this is the gospel we offer. It is not barren theory but spiritual reality, evidenced in hundreds of thousands of lives. Therefore (4:1) "we do not lose heart." How can we? Instead, we are more strongly urged to insure that our task of delivering the letter is done as Christ intends. Paul renews his commitment, and we must renew ours as well (4:2—3), to renounce any deception or distortion in ministering the word of God and to insure that by "setting forth the truth plainly" we "commend ourselves to every man's conscience in the sight of God."

Barriers to overcome

Because we might get carried away with the euphoric expectation that all we had to do was to preach the word faithfully and the Spirit would bring every hearer to life, Paul reminds us of the opposition. We have an enemy, of whom Paul has already spoken in connection with the Israelites in 3:13—16. He is (4:4) "the god of this age," who brings a blindness to the minds of unbelievers. Though the light of the gospel shines both in the lives of believers and in their sharing of the gospel message, the result can be negative. Eyes may see, but minds are blinded. Other philosophies guard the mind's door, prejudice jams it shut, sin rusts the lock and the hinges, ignorance blocks out the light.

Unless we understand this barrier to salvation, we might blame the gospel. Many have sought to adapt the gospel to suit modern man. But that is hopeless; it is not the gospel that needs changing.

I was traveling through Austria and the road ran suddenly into a road tunnel. It was a bright sunny day outside, but once in the tunnel I could not see. I panicked for a moment, and I blamed the Austrian roadbuilders. Then I remembered—I had my sunglasses on! There was nothing wrong with the tunnel—only with my ability to see. So it is with the gospel. The barriers that have to be removed are not in the gospel but in man.

As Calvin explains: "The blindness of unbelievers in no way detracts from the clearness of his gospel, for the sun is no less resplendent because the blind do not perceive its light."

Let there be light

The veil (3:16), the blindness imposed by the Enemy, is taken away only when a person turns to the Lord. That veil rests on everybody outside Christ.

Thus we have a further incentive to get on with the task of preaching Christ. There is no more urgent task. Only through faith in him can the veil be removed and the blindness be taken away. Although not every preaching of Christ will bring results, we are reminded that it *is* the only way results can come. So we are encouraged to preach "not ourselves but Jesus Christ as Lord" (4:5), and we are reminded that the God we are serving is the same God who brought light into the world in the mighty act of creation (4:6). Reaching into the hearts of unbelievers is a small thing by comparison— after all, he shone into *our* hearts and has opened us up to know him!

With such incentives we are prepared, with Paul, to be servants of others (4:5) with the gospel, for the sake of Jesus. And we have no greater privilege than to serve Christ in this way.

Peace

Questions for Study and Discussion

1. How do we know when we have "heard the call of God" for a particular direction in ministry? What are the Biblical criteria for success in God's eyes?

2. How does Colossians 1:15—18 compare with our human tendency to compartmentalize our Christian faith and neatly set it aside as "one part" or "an aspect" of our lives? What changes can we expect in those attitudes when Christ is truly "pre-eminent" in our lives?

3. What are the marks of a "peddler" of the truth? What kind of peddlers are at work in the church today?

4. What does "witnessing for Christ" mean to most people? What does "having the fragrance of Christ" mean? Are the two related? Discuss.

Fragrance Tells all
What kind of fragrance am I giving off?

CHAPTER 4

AT HOME OR AWAY

4:7—5:8

THE CHRISTIAN LIVES in a constant state of tension between the present and the future. We have become children of God through faith in Christ Jesus, but we still live in the world. We look forward to the redemption of our bodies, but for the moment we still live in them. Sin's dominion over our bodies is broken, but the sinful nature is still there. Freedom from pain, sorrow, and tears awaits us in heaven, but here on earth we still suffer with them. We are citizens of heaven but also citizens of earth. We are pilgrims on our way to the promised land, but we walk through the heat of the world's desert as we travel.

Some Christians want heaven now. They believe in sinless perfection and in bodily wholeness. They expect freedom from pain and trouble, claiming all the heavenly promises now. Others want to withdraw from the world

and try to live in separated groups. Paul is a strong oppo-
nent of any such ideas! He believes in the power of God
to change us and to heal, but he never promises total
freedom from all sin and all sickness.

When heaven does touch us and thrill us, these experiences encourage us on in this earthly pilgrimage. Paul
helps us come to terms both with our humanity and with
the glory ahead. The Christian way does not allow one to
be subjugated to the other but holds both together, richly
and fully. The false apostles in Corinth had taught the
Corinthians to despise Paul because of the sufferings he
was enduring. From the safety of the fellowship in Corinth they taught that real Christianity means freedom
from suffering. But Paul, working in the world with
courage and fervor for the cause of Christ, knows the
reality of pain, deprivation, danger, and persecution (he
later lists many of these experiences in 11:21ff). Like the
Corinthians, twentieth-century Christians need to be
warned of the false teachings that abound and to be prepared to discern and accept the truth of the gospel.

Fragile—handle with care! (4:7)
We have been uplifted by Paul in the previous verses so
that glory seems only a step away, and we can rightly
exalt in the Christian faith. We can say "Amen" to his
vivid description of the work of the Spirit and of his
transformation in our lives. We can be freshly filled with
joy as we realize that the God who created the world has
shone his light into our hearts. We are awed and
humbled by the privilege we have, not just to know about
Christ but to know him. This is "treasure." But "we have
this treasure in jars of clay." Only in the future will the
treasure be in a new resurrection body and freed from

all the limitations of sin. For the moment the treasure of Christ resides in this earthly frame—this "jar of clay."

Jars of clay are common in the east, even in this day of plastics and unbreakable materials. There are thousands of cheap clay jars, put to every possible use, and they are easily breakable. If you apply pressure to one, it will crack. If you drop one, it will shatter. Yet it can effectively contain all sorts of things. The "clay vessel" is an apt picture of the human body. The potential use of the body is enormous, but it is easily breakable. Pressure will crack it. A fall will break it. It is fragile.

We should accept this fragility and not fight against it. We can keep our bodies fit and well; we can develop skills and abilities. Yet we must beware of over-exerting our bodies and thinking that, because we are in Christ's service, we can do without adequate sleep, or food, or relaxation. Jesus knew the need for times apart, times of rest and refreshment.

A young woman once came to see me. She was a fine worker in the church, serving with much energy and faithfulness. However, she had begun to fray around the edges. She was not sleeping properly, and had become edgy and irritable. When I talked with her I found that she had no planned relaxation. The biblical concept of "redeeming the time" had been interpreted by her as not wasting a single moment in relaxation. I explained to her that at the end of a hard day, around 10 P.M., I needed to be released from all the concerns of the day. Often, I told her, the television was the quickest means of unwinding. She was startled. "You actually watch TV?" she asked. She had not come to terms with the fragility of her body; when she learned to relax she found again her freshness in Christ's service.

At times we must shut the door and be alone. At All Souls Langham Place we close the church completely the week after Christmas and give the staff a week off. After the enormous pressure through the fall, a complete break to refresh us for the demands of the new year is essential. Complaints come from outsiders; some expect us to work all the time, never relaxing. We must not be pushed by them.

Fragile but amazingly useful (4:7)
Paul recognizes that our fragility is an advantage in the service of Christ. When the treasure is evident even in jars of clay, then the glory is to God. He may well have been short and less than handsome. Several times in Scripture allusions are made to his appearance and manner of speech as if others tended to despise his physical experience. Because the treasure is in a jar of clay, we can see more readily that all the conversions, missionary successes, churches established in numerous towns and cities, the survival of long and dangerous journeys, the power in preaching, are from God and not just from Paul himself.

As I was giving the farewell address for a missionary returning to northern India, I was struck afresh by her apparent fragility. She was not outwardly attractive, not a person who commanded a second glance on the street. Yet she was returning to North India to serve Christ. Her many years of service testified to amazing courage, enterprise, and vision, yet she told of her experiences with a touch of humor that tended to minimize the power of the Holy Spirit in her work. In human terms, her return might appear to be a waste of money, but God would use her and work powerfully through her. The treasure was housed in a jar of clay, and the glory would be the Lord's.

There are not many wise, powerful, or noble in the service of Christ. Instead, says Paul in 1 Corinthians 1, God has chosen the foolish to shame the wise, the weak to shame the strong, the low and despised to bring to nothing things that are, so that "no human being may boast in the presence of God."

Years ago I was a leader at a boys' camp. The leadership team contained some outstanding people—fine athletes, strong men, and very intelligent and gifted people from the top universities. The evening talks, given by each leader in turn, were usually excellent. But one night the talk was quite embarrassing. The leader was nervous, hesitant, mixed up his words, stumbled through his talk. In human terms it was a disaster, and the rest of us hardly knew where to look during the message. Yet that night God reached through to the boys; many of them came to real faith or began to seek earnestly. The "all-surpassing power" was clearly from God and not from the speaker. God had used the man's fragility and the result was glorifying to himself.

Not exuberance but endurance (4:8—9)

Once we understand the principle of verse 7 we can face life in a different way. We see the experiences of life, the sufferings and the pressures, as opportunities through which we may glorify God. We do not spend our time pleading with God to take away all the sufferings and persecutions. If they are removed, wonderful! But if not, they provide an opportunity for God's power to be shown in our inadequacy. Paul expresses this principle vividly in Philippians 1 as he faces the possibility of imminent martyrdom. His one desire is to glorify Christ whether in the way he dies or in further service in his life on earth.

Second Corinthians 4 describes four experiences: hard pressed (*thlipsis* again), perplexed, persecuted, struck down. Apart from persecution, all are common experiences in life, familiar to all people. There is rarely a family that has not experienced problems, pressures, or sudden illness. Although the Christian is not delivered from all suffering, some people want to be. How often someone says, "Why has that happened to her? She was such a good Christian." But if Christians were exempt from trouble, everyone would embrace Christianity as an insurance against problems and illness! The scriptural view is utterly different: we share these experiences, but it is how we handle them that makes the difference.

As we face difficulties, the power of Christ works in us. We are *not* crushed, nor driven to despair, nor destroyed. In persecution we know we are not abandoned. If we live or die we are the Lord's; we are sustained by the hope set before us; we are able to come to our Father in prayer; we know that even if men destroy our bodies they cannot destroy our souls. Christ's grace is with us when we are being persecuted for him—just as Stephen, while the crowd was stoning him to death, could see Jesus "standing at the right hand of God."

A beach-hockey game was in vigorous progress during a Christian young people's retreat. One of the players was a girl who had taken Romans 8:28 as a truth for her life—that "all things work together for good for those who love God and are called according to his purpose." Suddenly, an enthusiastic swing of the hockey stick by another player caught her in the face. Teeth were smashed, blood poured from her mouth, her lips swelled like balloons, and her face was scratched and bruised. As we rushed to get medical attention she could hardly speak, but managed to say "Romans 8:28!"

The truth of the word was demonstrated that day. Several girls came to faith in Christ by seeing how Angela coped with that situation; just recently I met one of those girls, now a mature woman, still growing in Christ. Here was a person "struck down but not destroyed" and the power of God was a visible witness to others.

When we face a perplexing challenge and do not know how to tackle what seems to be an impossible situation, do we sit down and give up? Not if we follow Paul. Instead, we get on our knees and spend time with the Lord, bringing the situation to him. As we consider alternative solutions, we pray for his way through. When Jesus is our Lord we do not despair, but trust that he has a way through for his glory, even when we wait a long time before his way is shown. Often there are unseen factors that must be reconciled before the Lord can open the door on the problem. When he does open the door we may be able to see the reason for the delay.

The testimonies of those persecuted and imprisoned for Christ demonstrate this truth. The love for their captors, the way in which the presence of the Lord becomes intensely real, the deep work in their souls, revealing him in a new way, the greater and higher hope of life eternal —all these are their testimonies. Peter, in 1 Peter 4:13—15 says: "Rejoice that you participate in the sufferings of Christ, so that you may be overjoyed when his glory is revealed. If you are insulted because of the name of Christ, you are blessed, for the Spirit of glory and of God rests upon you ... if you suffer as a Christian, do not be ashamed, but praise God that you bear that name." As Christians we demonstrate the power and grace of God to be sufficient in the midst of any circumstances we face in this fallen world.

A matter of life and death (4:10—12)

In Colossians 3 we are urged to put to death our earthly nature and to put on the nature of God, because we have died with Christ and are risen again with him. In 2 Corinthians 4 we are urged to let circumstances be a means to that same end. The pressures and perplexities of life are an opportunity to further the death of the old nature and to foster the growth of the new nature; an opportunity to die to self and rise with Christ; an opportunity to know more of the death and the life of Jesus in ourselves.

Amy Carmichael of Dohnavur had learned this truth. She regarded the pain of malicious gossip as a means to die more to self. The further we go in the Christian life the more we see ourselves as we really are; our desire to die to self and be truly alive in Christ must increase. Like Paul, we must learn not to sweep the events of life to one side while our "Christian life" goes on in peace, but rather to bring the events of daily living into the transforming process. The pruning goes on and on, yet the results of good pruning are seen in greater fruitfulness and more glorious blossoms.

Pride may often be a barrier to such a work in our souls. We do not want to lose face with other Christians; we want to appear to others better than we know ourselves to be; we want to hear others say how great we are; often we want to deceive ourselves. Pride has to be broken down before we can open to God's transformation through life's experiences. The breaking of that pride in Peter brought him to openness, making his first letter a marvelous expression of how to face and use suffering.

Are we prepared to humble ourselves under the mighty hand of God? Are we prepared to let him knock off the sharp corners and work deeply in the festering swamps of our sinful natures?

Once I was a choirboy. The choirmaster, intent on improving the voices of another chorister and myself, asked us to go to his home one evening. When we found out that it was the last evening for seeing a film about a haunted house at the local theater we were very upset. We went to the choirmaster's house with dragging feet, but he was not there when we arrived. Hope sprang in our hearts! Time ticked on; he was delayed at some other meeting. Finally we managed to persuade his wife that he would be very tired when he came home. She let us go and we ran and ran. Our glance down a darkened side street gave us a sight of the choirmaster hurrying towards his home—but we rushed on to the cinema for the film (which was terrible!). The real trouble with us was that we did not *want* to have our voices changed and improved. It was not important to us, and lesser things took priority. Likewise, in the Christian life, the real question is: Do we *want* to be changed? If so, then we will ponder these verses in 2 Corinthians 4 until they are part of our thinking and thus of our growing in the death and life of Christ. If not, we will be content with lesser things.

Deliverance is also a cause for glory (4:13—15)

As much as Paul sees the value of suffering (both here and in Romans 5: "Suffering produces perseverance;

perseverance, character; and character, hope"), he also
sees that glory abounds to God in deliverance. In the
present circumstances he believes God is going to bring
about a deliverance which will bring benefit to the Corinthians and cause much thanksgiving. Paul is never in any
doubt that God is always able to deliver, to heal, to act.
He believes in the God "who raised Jesus from the dead."
That same God could deliver Paul from his present circumstances and bring him safely to the Corinthians.

We must not get so carried away with the blessings of
suffering, or with the glory to God in enduring pressures
and perplexities, that we forget to be open to the possibility of release, healing, or restoration. Paul's outlook is
balanced: he wants the glory of God. Because that is his
overriding aim, he is prepared to let God work out the
way in which the glory is to be expressed.

Those who feel that God can only be glorified by total
deliverance or healing are obstructing God's purpose.
Similarly, those who feel there can be no special healing
or deliverance are also hindering God's purposes.
Rather, we should be open to either, with faith and submission to God. Like Chrysostom, who endured much
persecution, we should say, "Glory to God in all things.
Amen!" When the way is deliverance, when a believer is
released from imprisonment for their faith, when someone is healed, or when a way through a problem is
opened up clearly and marvelously by the Lord, we can
celebrate, and thanksgiving can abound to the glory of
God (v. 15). Yet we must also praise and thank God for
his glory worked out in those who are not released or
not healed or who do not have the way opened up clearly
—and yet who turn this to God's glory.

An eternal perspective is good for you! (4:16—18)
The old jibe about Christians being so heavenly-minded
that they are of no earthly use is easily thrown at us—but
just as easily rebuffed. For some, of course, the criticism
is sadly applicable. But for most Christians, being heavenly-minded inspires us to be more useful in this life. If
the accusation sometimes makes us feel a little ashamed
of any thoughts about heaven or eternity, these verses
should grip our souls. Paul was constantly inspired by
what lay ahead and found great strength from the eternal perspective in his life. It affects all our values, our
ambitions, our attitudes—and thrills us as well!

The first contrast that Paul draws is between the outer
and the inner. Our outer fabric, our body, is in irreversi-
ble decay. We can keep the decaying work in check wherever possible, keeping our bodies as attractive and fit as
possible. But the decoration and jogging and slimming is
really a losing battle. The body is decaying and will one
day return to dust.

Yet the real person can be renewed every day! In spite
of wrinkles, fading eyesight, and decreased energy, the
soul can keep young and fresh, maturing with new in-
sight into the things of God and no decrease of inward
power.

People without hope in Christ tend to grow old inwardly as well as outwardly, but the Christian has the
Holy Spirit within, new life day by day. True believers in
their old age, still eager to learn more of Jesus, still
wanting to grow in the knowledge of him and of his
word, manifest the fruit of the Holy Spirit in their loving
lives. I was deeply moved by a group of elderly believers
living in the Mowll Retirement Village in Australia. They

were at the CMS Summer School where I was speaking. After each session they would come and clutch my hand, tears of gratitude in their eyes, praising God for what they had learned that evening in the talk, longing to know more of him.

But not all elderly Christians are like that, and the reason appears in verse 16. The renewal "day by day" is not automatic, but comes only for those who seek that daily renewal, who feed on the word and learn to meditate, who practice devotional prayer fellowship with their Lord day by day, who long to grow in Christ. Whatever our age, this fellowship is vital to renewal. Renewal is not unique to one movement or one special segment of Christianity. It is the birthright of every believer and is possible and intended for every believer—if we don't throw it away by laziness or preoccupation with other responsibilities.

The second contrast is between the present light and momentary troubles and the weighty glory of eternity. This life is really very short—sixty, seventy, eighty years —sometimes more, sometimes less, but nothing when compared with eternity. As Calvin said: "A moment is long if we look at the things around us, but once we have raised our minds to heaven, a thousand years begin to be like a moment." There is simply no comparison, says Paul, between the short time in this fallen world and all that God has prepared for those who love him. So whenever the going gets rough, we can lift our eyes and get a glimpse of glory ahead; we can stand on the spiritual mountain-top and look across to the mighty peaks of heaven. When we arrive, the journey back on earth will seem so short, and the great human aims and glories on earth will seem petty and paltry compared with the glory of heaven.

The third contrast is between what is seen, which is temporary, and what is unseen, which is eternal. Jesus told us not to lay up treasure on earth, but to lay up treasure in heaven. The materialistic world sets great store by wealth, luxury, fame and success. The Christian, influenced by these attitudes, has to work out a lifestyle for living in the world while preparing for eternity. What the world prizes is temporary, geared only to this world, but the true values of life and love, of sharing and caring, of worship and fellowship, are with us forever. We must constantly "fix our eyes" not on the seen but on the unseen. This change of perspective is not achieved in a moment, but is, rather, a constant refixing of our eyes, a constant adjustment in our navigating perspective.

You are on your way home (5:1—5)

If our homes are really "home," then we look forward to returning after a journey or a vacation. Before summer vacation we limp along, looking forward to getting away and then, on vacation, we thoroughly enjoy being apart from the pressures of normal working life. But after two or three weeks we begin to look forward to going home. Paul thinks of heaven in those terms—not that we will then be away, but that we are away now and then will be home (v. 8).

When we are still young and thoughts of eternity are fairly remote, we probably anticipate life on earth; but as we get older the perspective changes. Paul is enormously confident about the prospect of going home. In 5:1 he says "we know" (that is, we have come to understand and grasp with conviction), and in 5:6 "we are always confident."

The unbeliever will readily chide us for such confidence. While visiting a family for a meal, our youngest son, in his early teens at the time, was describing his delight at visiting Disneyland. "When I get to heaven," he said, "I want to thank Mr. Disney for creating Disneyland." The mother of the family we were visiting turned on him, and with scorn and acidity mocked him for his confidence about going to heaven. He was startled, but unmoved.

Such confidence comes, of course, from the promises of God and the resurrection of Jesus. There is, however, a restlessness in the Christian's heart, a sense of anticipation, a feeling that much more lies ahead, a sense that a far greater life is in store, a longing to have the resurrection body and freedom from this earthly one. This restlessness, this tension between what is and what will be, is a result of the Holy Spirit's indwelling. Indeed, the very restlessness is a sign of the Spirit being within us, for the unspiritual person has no such tension or longing other than a vague hope. If he thinks about heaven at all, it is only as an afterthought to this life, not the glorious destiny of the redeemed. We can bathe in the wonder of verse 5: "It is God who has made us for this very purpose." That is our destiny!

The Holy Spirit is the deposit (v. 5), the down-payment, the first installment, the pledge of what is to come. We touch and experience glory by his indwelling, always knowing that this is but the hem of the garment, the foretaste of the fullness to come.

At home with the Lord

Supremely, going home means going home not to a place but to a person. This is true in human families—the long-distance telephone calls, the letters, the longing to be reunited with loved ones, the moment of crossing the threshold and being greeted with open arms of love. How much more is that going to be true when we go home to the Lord! At the moment, although we have his indwelling and his presence with us, we are still, in Paul's terms "away from the Lord" (v. 6). But when this earthly life ceases, when the earthly body is left behind, when the fallen world has dropped away from us, we shall come to him. Whatever heaven may be like (and it will be glorious!) the center of it all will be the Lord himself. We shall be at home with the Lord, and with all who love him, forever!

Questions for Study and Discussion

1. Discuss how the analogy of "treasure in jars of clay" serves both as an encouragement and as a warning for Christians. How can human weakness be an opportunity for a manifestation of the glory of God?

2. What misunderstandings about God arise from the belief that it is always his will to heal or deliver?

3. Discuss what it means, and what it takes, to be "renewed inwardly" by the Holy Spirit.

4. How does the prospect of eternal life with Christ affect the way we live our daily lives on earth?

CHAPTER 5

AMBASSADOR OR PASSENGER?

5:9—6:13

THE FLAME OF ETERNAL HOPE was fanned into a blazing fire by the previous verses. Glory filled the horizon. Without any apology, Paul encouraged us to revel in our eternal destiny of being "at home with the Lord."

But the prospect of heaven ahead must be applied to service in the present. Not only will we come into our heavenly inheritance, but we will come before Christ with the life he gave us to live for him on earth, reporting back, looking at what we have done for him. Paul develops this theme into a major attack upon the Corinthians' lack of evangelistic concern and urges them, with the passion of a heart committed to evangelism, to get into action, regardless of possible persecution and physical hardship. They are to prove themselves as genuine servants of God.

Goal! (5:9)

What is the greatest goal, ambition, aim of life? Paul has one supreme goal—to please Christ. This will be his aim when he is at home with the Lord and it is his ambition while he is still away from the Lord. The thin line between life on earth and life in heaven does not interrupt this overriding ambition.

Does this mean that we cannot have other ambitions in life? Is it wrong to want to win at sports, to succeed in examinations, or to get promotions in our jobs? Not at all. Christians in positions of success and influence can often be effectively used for Christ. Yet if such positions are what we most want in life we have our priorities wrong. Success carries with it responsibility to others, but particularly to God.

Earthly ambitions are fine as long as they are submitted to Christ. In such submission we often find Christ requiring us to take a role that may never appear successful in human terms, to go across the world to serve in some obscure yet needy area, to be "behind the scenes" in some work for him. If we are prepared to abandon worldly success for the cause of Christ, then we can handle human ambitions of any kind, because over and above them will be the ambition to please him.

The goal is to please him. Our Lord and Savior has done much for us; the only logical response to his mercy and love is the surrender of our lives—to give back our bodies to him as a living sacrifice (Rom. 12:1—2), not to a "cause" but to a person.

When I was called into the Army at eighteen I was sent first to a training camp in the north of England. At first we all resented the discipline and the constant shouting of orders. Then we were transferred to another section and placed under an Irish sergeant-major who immediately won our love and respect. Every soldier on the barrack square wanted the parade to be perfect—for him. We did not want to let him down; when at one point the howling wind prevented some from hearing the order to "about face" and half the troup went one way and half the other way, we were all terribly upset. We had let down this sergeant-major who meant so much to us. We had no ambition to present a perfect passing-out parade for its own sake—but we did for his sake.

In the same way, the living of a life of love and service for its own sake—or to fulfill a standard of law—is not likely to inspire us. But living a life of love and service for Christ, who has saved us and loves us, transforms the situation. When we fail, we let him down. When we do not bother to serve, we grieve his heart. When we are obedient to his direction we bring joy to his heart.

Often I feel that it would be good to do some other job, or to have the opportunity to have a different sort of ministry, or to achieve what some others achieve, or to have different gifts to use, or to be in a different place and a different sphere of influence. But then I am re-called to the fact that I am the servant of Christ and my greatest aim is to be where he wants me to be, to do what he wants me to do, when he wants me to do it.

Criticism is always hard to take, particularly if we are sensitive. We may be told that we should be exercising this gift or that ministry, or that our method of evange-lism is not the best way, and some other church is up-lifted as the pattern. We cannot reject criticism; we must weigh it. But in the end we are answerable to God. We have to be God-pleasers, not man-pleasers. We must be fully persuaded in our own minds that the course of action, the form of ministry, the strategic plan, is the Lord's, and we must not be swayed from it by the extolling of what happens elsewhere. Christ is the head of the Church, and our ambition must be to please him.

The judgment seat (5:10—13)

The judgment seat of Christ is the judging-place of Christians, not the judgment of eternal salvation. That is an issue settled by our faith in Christ as Savior. Paul is in no doubt about that, as the rest of this chapter shows (v. 19).

In 1 Corinthians 3:11—15, Paul makes clear that there is only one foundation, Jesus Christ. That foundation stands all tests; what we build on the foundation, however, is going to be tested by fire. He contrasts the lasting value of gold, silver, and precious stones with the short-lived wood, hay, or straw. On the Day of the Lord the quality of our work for Christ will be tested, says Paul. Will it survive the test because it has been really worthwhile or will it disappear in smoke because it has been useless and shallow? It is a somber and challenging contrast to ponder. 1 Corinthians 3:15 then makes sure we do not get the salvation implication wrong. If our work is burned up we will suffer loss but we "will be saved." So the judgment seat, before which "we must all appear" (2 Corinthians 5:10), where everything will be in the open, judges how we have built on the foundation since we became part of his family through faith.

Christ will look at our lives in practical terms, at "things done while in the body" (v. 10). It is the body that acts, serves, sits with the ill, visits the prisoners, scrubs floors, cooks meals, moves chairs, cares for the elderly, makes coffee, provides hospitality, befriends the outcast, runs camps, goes across the world or the street or the corridor to serve others. It is the body that is to be a clean vessel for Christ to use, not caught up with the world's marring and lowering of the image of God in man, nor involved in bestiality, sadism, cruelty, or promiscuity. It is with the body that we think, study, speak and converse. It is with the body that we can be helpful or hurtful. It is with the body that we serve Christ now.

Although every believer will share in salvation and thus in eternal life, there is clearly a difference in the recognition by Christ of what has or has not been done for him, as Jesus indicated in his parable of the talents. His "Well done, good and faithful servant" will be worth everything—all the years of service and action for him. His disappointment at our failure to use our life fruitfully for him will be like a stab-wound—we will wish that we could go back and re-live our lives. It will be too late then, so we must learn the lesson now. We must aim for the crown, aim to run so that we may win.

Paul responds on his own part with fresh zeal in evangelism. When he speaks of the fear of the Lord (v. 11) causing him to persuade others with the gospel, he is not thinking of their judgment but of his own. He uses "fear" in the sense of "awe." There is indeed a great awesomeness about our facing Christ, and we should never treat service for Christ lightly or casually. I find the pulpit a place of awe and joy.

When I entered the ministry, I was rapidly delivered from the fear of preaching to large crowds. The vast congregations at All Souls soon did not worry me. Yet I have become increasingly burdened with the awe of God, the awe of handling his word and being the messenger of God to so many people. I do not want to let him down and I find it hard to be at peace with myself if I feel I have not handled the word as well as he wanted and as well as I ought to have done.

What is true of the pulpit is true of any service for him —we must not be casual about preparation for a Sunday school class, a Bible study group, organizing visitation, counseling, even the many practical tasks of Christian service, in the kitchen, maintaining the premises, or participation in committees.

We must also beware of judging others by what is seen. The Corinthians did that (v. 12) and apparently formed a wrong judgment. In the final analysis it is God who judges perfectly, as he sees the heart. "What we are is plain to God" (v. 11); even if (v. 13) others think him out of his mind in his service for Christ (Jesus' relatives thought this about him), Paul does not swerve because, he says, "if we are out of our mind it is for the sake of God"!

Love is compelling (5:13—15)

Action is stirred by the thought of Christ's judgment seat; it is compelled by the thought of Christ's love. Paul is not referring to our love for Christ but to Christ's love for us. The *agape* of God is central here. There is a form of love for Christ that is sustained by fresh fervor in rallies, meetings and services—it needs to be worked up and maintained constantly. Those who depend on such emotion become depressed when they do not feel that love, and go into spiritual "highs" when they do feel it.

Stability only comes when we see that Christ's love for us is a fact—a fact of history, and a fact of our personal history if we have believed on him. The fact of the cross will never alter. It will be a fact tomorrow, and the next day, and the next day, and forever. God intends that every believer should come to a more profound understanding of the meaning of the cross—and thus, of his love for us. Romans 5:5 confirms this: "God has poured out his love into our hearts by the Holy Spirit." The Holy Spirit wants us to understand and experience his love for us; He makes this love in the cross real to us.

The cross is at the center of Paul's heart. He has pondered long and deep on the significance of Christ's crucifixion, and the Holy Spirit has been his illuminator. We must ponder the cross, too, and like Paul, be "convinced that one died for all." The word "convinced" implies an idea that is thought through. The tense of the verb indicates not a developing idea, but a conviction firmly established and influencing one's whole life.

There are those who teach that the cross is primarily an example of God's love to inspire us; or that it is the supreme evidence of what evil wants to do to good. Both these ideas are helpful, but neither is the major meaning of the cross in the Bible. There is overwhelming biblical testimony that the cross is God's taking our place and taking the penalty we deserve as sinners. "One died for all," the "substitutionary atonement." Those who call this a barbaric theory or a heathen idea are attacking a warped version of substitution, not the biblical one. Unless we grasp the truth of Christ's dying in our place we can never know real assurance of salvation. Those who try to discredit substitutionary atonement also discredit the idea of man being able to have assurance of salvation. The two are linked together.

A clergyman once brought the issue to a head in his church by saying in the middle of his sermon: "Stand up if you know you are saved." There was an enormous furor afterwards. "How dare those people stand up—the presumptuousness of saying they are saved—nobody can know that until the day of judgment." They were sincere, yet they were missing the point. Those who say they are saved are not doing so because they "presumptuously" think they are good enough for God but because they do not think they can ever be good enough for God. Their trust is in Jesus Christ who died for them, taking the penalty of their sin and declaring them his children forever.

The "presumptuous" people are actually those who reckon that in the day of judgment they will be all right because they will have lived lives good enough for God. Their trust is in themselves, not in the Savior of the world. They see their so-called good deeds as their passport to heaven. Because they do not see themselves as lost sinners they do not see the point or need of Christ dying in their place on the cross.

Salvation is the most important issue for any human being. Where is your trust for salvation? Is it in Jesus or yourself? Do you believe that he died for you and that therefore you have died and been raised to new life in Christ? He died for all, says Paul—for everyone in the world, in every generation. No one is excluded from the possibility of salvation. "Therefore all died" means that Christ died as the representative of the whole human race. There is no universalism here—everyone will not be saved—but the *offer* of salvation is universal. We must receive and believe to make it our own.

Vital as this truth is to grasp and ponder, Paul declares it here as a spur to evangelism and service for Christ, a compulsion. "Christ's love compels us." The word means holding together, pressing together, hemming in.

The late Alan Stibbs illustrated this verse by his experience traveling by boat along a Chinese river. The river was sluggish as it went across the flat plains, but when it came to a narrow gorge, the waters tumbled and roared with such great force that the passengers had to hold on tightly. The power came when the waters were hemmed in, Stibbs said. So in the Christian life, only as our hearts and lives are hemmed in by the love of Christ on the cross can we begin to have real power in service. We are left no choice. The compulsion is such that "those who live should no longer live for themselves but for him who died for them and was raised again" (v. 15). A revolution takes place!

Sometimes commitment to Christ's service becomes listless and casual; we begin to live for ourselves, for our pleasure, for our own profit. As we come to a worship service, especially the communion service, in which the cross is central, we ponder the cross afresh, and it becomes a searchlight to our souls, compelling us to rededicate our souls and bodies as a living sacrifice in Christ's service. The cross constantly challenges the bias we have towards living for self and inspires us to bold and vigorous living for Christ.

New birth has surprising effects! (5:16—17)

The text "if anyone is in Christ he is a new creation" is frequently quoted out of context. Its dynamic truth is taught in many other parts of the Bible, and we know its meaning in our lives, for the Holy Spirit brought us to rebirth and has begun to change us. But Paul states this truth at this point in his letter as an incentive to evangelism and service for Christ.

In verse 16 we see two effects of this new creation: the

first, that "from now on we regard no one from a worldly point of view." Before we come to Christ we judge people from a "worldly point of view." We judge by outward success, intelligence, physique, position, wealth and achievement. Then, when we come to Christ, we find ourselves beginning to see people differently. We begin to see through the masks and the plastic exteriors and to see into the heart of people. The Lord looks on the heart, not at the outward appearance, and the Holy Spirit helps us to see as he sees. The wealthy executive wielding power but having no peace or purpose for living becomes someone to pity and to reach for Christ. The pop star whose music is acclaimed, whose skill with the guitar is marvelous, whose records sell millions, and before whom the fans go wild with frenzied adoration; yet who is desperately lonely, sick of luxury, consumed by drugs, and suicidal, is to be pitied. He needs Christ; life is meaningless without Christ. All the riches and fame this world can load upon man can never satisfy the human heart.

So the "new creation" believer finds himself looking past the façade. His relatives may be a wonderful family, but if they are without Christ, he cannot but be concerned to pray, love, and witness. As we mix with people day after day we cannot but see them as Jesus did, as "sheep without a shepherd." Prejudices and barriers break down. The Christ who broke the barriers between Jew and Gentile, slave and free, male and female, is the Christ who does not see the color of the skin or the cultural background of a person. Nor should we. The new creation enables the Christian to see other people as Jesus sees them, not from a worldly point of view.

The second effect is that we see Christ differently:

"Though we once regarded Christ in this way, we do so no longer" (v. 16). We no longer perceive him from a "worldly point of view," regarding him just as a man— possibly a very special man, but just a man. The new creation reveals Christ as Lord and God, head of creation and head of the church, Savior of the world, eternal King.

A woman I corresponded with had rejected Jesus Christ and the Christian faith, but gradually by correspondence and reading she came into a real faith. After a while she wrote: "That I could ever have dared to approach God as 'some vague abstract higher intelligence,' seeking his voice and guidance while simultaneously denying Jesus as Lord and Savior together with his gospel of love, is much too painful and distressing to verbalize." The new creation in her life brought her to see Jesus in an entirely different way.

The reverse is true, as well. Various theologians have written books denying the divinity of Christ. They may be sincere, but they also show that they have not met with Jesus nor experienced his new creation. They can only see Christ from a "wordly point of view."

These two changes in our thinking—about other people and about Christ—spur us to serve him. People everywhere need to be reached. We bring them not a human theory, but a gospel made possible through the eternal Son of God himself. We know it to be true because we experience this new creation. "The old has gone, the new has come"!

God is relying on you (5:18—21)

Once we are part of the new creation, God entrusts us with "the message of reconciliation" (v. 19). Nobody else can do it for him. Only believers, recipients of this reconciliation, this salvation, can possibly share it with others. So God relies on each of us to get on with the task for him. No angels will preach to your neighbor, no seraphic choir will announce the good news to your colleagues at work, no vision in the sky will declare the gospel to your relatives and friends. The message must come through human agency—through all who are "in Christ."

Quite often, in the area of London in which I lived, I saw the ambassadors of foreign countries setting off in the ceremonial car to present their credentials to the sovereign. The ambassador speaks for his country and for the leader of his country. He does not speak on his own behalf. When we act as "ambassadors for Christ," we speak in his name and not in our own name, "as though God were making his appeal through us" (v. 20) . . . "we implore on Christ's behalf." There is, incidentally, no "you" in the Greek. Paul is not pleading with the Corinthians to be reconciled, for they had already received Christ; rather, he is showing that the task of the ambassador is to implore others to be reconciled.

Reconciliation has taken place in Christ, dealing with the sins of mankind. We are to declare the truth and urge others to accept it: "Be reconciled to God." We cannot reconcile ourselves but we are to "be reconciled." In humility we must receive what he has done once and for all.

We need also to show how this was made possible— through Christ alone and what he did. Verse 21, described as the most profound verse in the Bible, gets to the heart of substitutionary atonement. It is not just that Christ bore sins, but that he *became* sin. Standing in awe on the edge of this truth, we hear the cry from the cross, "My God, my God, why have you forsaken me?" and sense something of the awful darkness that came upon Jesus in that terrible separation from the Father. Our wonder at this divine love is deepened when we see that he who became sin was himself without sin. There could be no greater contrast. Our attitude to sin is often so obscured that we can hardly appreciate what it meant for Christ the sinless to become sin. This amazing love had as its aim making us right with God. The reconciliation was made possible through Christ's once-for-all sacrifice. We who have received its salvation can surely have no greater privilege or expression of our thanksgiving than to be ambassadors for him with the glorious gospel of reconciliation.

Is God's grace in vain? (6:1—13)

After those closing verses of chapter 5 it seems impossible that Christians would ever grow complacent in their desire to reach others with the loving reconciliation of Christ. Yet when we look into our own hearts we know it can be so; it was certainly true of the Corinthians. They had become so turned in on themselves with their spiritual self-indulgence that evangelism had become of little importance. Hence, Paul's driving force of argument throughout chapter 5, which contains some of the greatest truths of scripture concerning the cross, is aimed at stirring the Corinthians into action.

Paul's final plea on this theme urges them "not to receive God's grace in vain." He does not plead with them to receive Christ, but rather not to sit back and do nothing about it. The words of verse 2 are often used as an evangelistic appeal: "Now is the time of God's favor, now is the day of salvation." But the real purpose is to stir the Corinthians to spread the gospel. Perhaps they were saying, "Well, let's enjoy and deepen our fellowship first and then we may think about evangelism." The time is always *now* for evangelism, not tomorrow or the next day —today is always the day, and Paul urges them not to throw away the opportunities of the present moment.

Paul has pointed the Corinthians to the judgment seat of Christ, to the compelling love of Christ, to their new attitude to people, and to the expectation of Christ for all of us to be ambassadors. His final thrust points to himself and those with him, to show what it means to serve Christ. He knows that the Corinthians will be told by the false apostles that Paul's effort is the energy of the flesh and human volition rather than God's way.

Thus Paul plunges into a succession of events and experiences, piling one upon another with breathless rapidity, leaving the unmistakable impression that here is a man on fire for God.

Before he lists the activities, he shows his concern not to be a stumbling block to others. Many people become so busy for Christ that their own spiritual growth stops and they begin to wither inwardly until their life becomes a barrier to the gospel. The "discrediting" of our ministry (v. 3) is a mocking, a ridicule, a despising of any disparity between word and life. As Denney put it: "People will be glad of an excuse not to listen to the gospel and will look for such in the conduct of ministers." Calvin says, "It is an artifice of Satan to seek some misconduct on the part of ministers which may tend to the dishonor of the gospel." Those who will be ambassadors for Christ cannot always avoid the bitter and ugly defamations or distorted condemnations that come; Jesus experienced such himself. But we can do our best to avoid what might give rise to such attacks.

In the list from verses 4—10 the overall quality shown is endurance. The fire of the amabassador's heart is not easily extinguished. Paul pressed on regardless of the opposition; he did not keep inside a cozy fellowship circle and do nothing.

It is possible to categorize the list to help us apply it to our own lives:

1. *Problems that come to us as they do to anybody in the world*—the troubles *(thlipsis* again), the hardships of poverty, illness, unemployment, the "distresses" of perplexity, sudden bereavement. All are opportunities to be an ambassador of the grace of Christ.

2. *The difficulties we may go through, simply because we are Christians.* For Paul, there were beatings, imprisonments, and riots. He endured terrible experiences, as have countless thousands of Christians through the centuries, in the cause of the gospel.

3. *Stresses that we cause ourselves by our work for the gospel.* Paul endured "hard work, sleepless nights, hunger." As ambassadors for Christ we are prepared to serve, and being a committed Christian demands very hard work and long hours!

4. *The fruit of the Spirit in action in our daily lives:* patience, love, truth, power, resistance to being disturbed by the fickle opinions of others.

5. *The spiritual alchemy that transforms situations by the power of Christ.* We may be regarded as people not worth knowing, but we are sure the Lord knows us; we are dead and useless in the eyes of society, but we know real life in Christ; we will not let our spirit be killed even though our body is beaten; we find joy in Christ as well as sorrow for the world; we are poor, perhaps, yet possessing everything! What a testimony! Paul certainly lived his life

in the triumphant grace of Christ—and he lived it in service for Christ.

Can the Corinthians still remain unmoved, closing their hearts to Paul, as the false apostles had influenced them to do? In spite of all the pain he feels, he loves them and has opened his heart wide to them. He longs that they might open wide their hearts, too.

Questions for Study and Discussion

1. What are some common motives—good and bad—for serving Christ? Why is God interested in our motivation as well as in the results of our service?

2. Why do many people want to earn or deserve salvation rather than accepting Christ's atoning work by faith?

3. Contrast the treasures of the world's system with the things considered valuable by those who walk by faith. Why does becoming a "new creation" in Christ effect such a drastic change in a person's value system?

4. In what ways do we fulfill the position of "ambassador for Christ"? As ambassadors, in what ways can we effectively represent Christ to the world around us?

CHAPTER 6

GODLY SEPARATION AND GODLY SORROW

6:14—7:16

OCCASIONALLY I RECEIVE A LETTER FROM a person who says he is leaving his church or denomination. Such people nearly always refer to this part of 2 Corinthians and claim that they are being obedient to God in that separation. Recently a woman wrote, urging me to "come out and be separate" until we both found the true church. The misuse of this Scripture is pernicious, and the position is usually held without any love; we must, therefore, look clearly and carefully at it.

Godly separation
The issue to grasp. The verses from 2 Corinthians 6:14 to 7:1 must be among the most misused in the Bible. They seem to form a segment of their own; some people think they are part of the letter referred to in 1 Corinthians

5:9. The truth being communicated, however, is a strong statement on "separation." It has been used by some as a reason for retreating away from other people into remote communities, or for separation even from other Christian groups who do not line up with what is considered necessary for the Christian life. Families have been broken up and friendships marred by a legalistic use of this passage.

The passage must be considered in the context of our Lord's requirements in John 17 that his disciples should be "in the world but not of the world." The fact of Christ becoming man, the Incarnation, implies a sharing in human life, not a separation from it. Yet the one who so readily ate with tax-collectors and sinners showed us also how to be separated to God and to keep close to the Father. Jesus did not make *deep* bonds of relationship with unbelievers even though he mixed freely with them and spoke to them of the faith. Similarly, we can see that it is *deep* bonds, permanent or semi-permanent relationships, which Paul is describing. He uses the word "yoked"; two animals joined together in the task of pulling a plough or a cart must keep closely in step and be closely identified in a common task and purpose.

The inequality. Paul suggests inequality with this picture of two animals entirely unsuited to each other yet yoked together, as in Deuteronomy 22:10, where the yoking of an ox and a donkey is forbidden. Paul demonstrates the total inequality between an unbeliever and a believer if they are in a close personal bond. Righteousness and wickedness are utterly opposite to each other; they cannot mix—they are on entirely different planes of thought and action. Light and darkness cannot mix; the in-between twilight is neither one nor the other.

In Ephesians 5:8 Paul reminds us that light in the Lord should not only *avoid* darkness but *expose* the works of darkness. The two are at war, and no compromise can be contemplated. Paul presses the point further by contrasting Christ and Belial, referring to Satan, although the word means "worthless." How can someone under bondage to Satan mix with someone under the lordship of Christ? As Jesus said, "No man can serve two masters."

This argument of total incompatibility or inequality obviously refers to close liaisons and committed relationships—marriage, business partnerships, close friendships, and employment—rather than to casual acquaintances. Often when I find myself counseling a Christian and a non-Christian who want to get married, I find they regard the spiritual aspect as of secondary importance. "Yes, she can go to church" and, "yes, she can send the children to Sunday School" and, "yes, she can take an interest in Christian things if she wants to . . ." as if it were all a matter of taste or fashion.

Yet the issue is far deeper. The person who turns to Christ, has the whole life and outlook changed and there is a willingness to go on being transformed. A marriage to a non-Christian will produce endless conflicts about the ambitions of life, the use of time and money, ethical actions, honesty and truth, the way Sunday is observed, facing matters with or without prayer, the use of the home, and how the children are brought up. The differences are as deep as the foundations; the Christian will be guided by the authority of the Word of God, the non-Christian by personal opinions, humanistic philosophies, or selfish motives.

Sometimes, of course, the non-Christian partner comes into a real faith in Christ. But there are more disasters than successes; usually the Christian is forced to compromise time after time and eventually loses the vitality of faith in the living God. The warning of Scripture and experience should be heeded by those contemplating a marriage that is "mixed" in the matter of faith. Both parties will be wounded, not just the believer.

In the world of commerce or, at the local level, of being an employee, the warning of this passage must also be heeded. A Christian may find himself forced to share in a dishonest act. One Christian I know was working for a brewery when he came to biblical faith. It was regular custom to handle one barrel a day dishonestly—to falsify records and to pocket the money. When he became a Christian, he refused to do this and no one would go on the truck with him. He was forced to change his job. Another Christian was involved, before conversion, in insurance swindles, arranging for flood damage to "happen" to stock that could no longer be sold. He refused to do this when he became a Christian and his employers reacted strongly.

The ethics of business are often regarded as different from any other ethics, and when a Christian applies the unchanging ethical standards of the Bible he is not welcome. Close business liaisons which are "unequal yoking" should be avoided. Differences, in marriage or other close relationships, over tastes, sports, color schemes, food, and the like are of secondary importance—they are areas of give and take. But the issues of the Spirit and of submission to Jesus Christ are not negotiable. Inequality at this level is an invitation to disaster.

The indwelling. In 1 Corinthians 3:16, Paul spoke of our bodies as temples and said that God's Spirit lives in us. Just as in Old Testament times there could be no compromise between heathen idols and the temple of God, so it is with us. Idols were lifeless, not hearing, not seeing, not walking (Psalm 115), the works of men's hands; but the living God is over all and does what he pleases. If we entertain heathen philosophies or the materialism of our modern world, we dishonor the living God who indwells us by his Spirit.

The promise that God would live with us and walk among us has been fulfilled in Christ by the Spirit. No other idols can be given house-room. A close liaison—a yoked partnership—with an unbeliever is a compromise, a rival to the lordship of Christ within us. When we find a friendship pulling us away, challenging Christ, exercising influence in a non-Christian way, involving us in actions, standards, or gatherings that are clearly anti-Christ or against his word, it is time to run. We need to break free, to come out and be separate. Where we are able to maintain relationships with unbelievers without compromise or threat to the lordship of Christ we should do so for the gospel's sake.

The implications. 2 Corinthians 7:1 emphasizes that reverence for God is at stake; nothing must rival him and our submission to him. There are two parts to this verse; the first is about specific matters and specific occasions. "Let us purify ourselves" appears in a Greek form that means an act of "purifying" happening many times as we meet each particular challenge. Perhaps we find ourselves in a party that we thought was going to be enjoyable but gradually we realize it is an impure gathering, against the word and the will of Christ. We must "purify ourselves" by leaving the party. A man longs for marriage, and at first the woman he meets seems wonderful. People think of them as "a couple," but he begins to find out things about her that are anything but Christian. Will his pride allow him to abandon the relationship? With any relationship that goes out of tune spiritually, "purify" means "act."

The other half of the verse indicates an on-going effect —a lifetime attitude which is steadily deepened and matured by the Spirit. The Christian's desire to grow in holiness, in reverence for God, is fed by the word, by prayer, by fellowship, by sharing in the life of the church, and by meditating on God and all he has done for us.

If we want to live godly lives, we will avoid all "that contaminates body and spirit." The promise in the last verse of chapter 6, one of a series of Old Testament references, is that God "will receive" us and "be a Father" to us. The testimony of hundreds of thousands of Christians across the centuries would witness to the truth of that promise; as we draw closer to him so he draws closer to us.

Godly Sorrow

Get loving! The new commandment of Jesus was to love one another so that all men would know that we are his disciples. The bonding together of all kinds of people into a fellowship of love is humanly inexplicable, a testimony of the work of the Spirit of God. The power of such testimony is not merely diminished if we do not love one another; rather, lack of love confirms the unbeliever in his cynicism towards the Christian's claims of new life.

Paul is deeply concerned, therefore, that love abound among Christians; the rift between himself and the Corinthians hurts him. Their hearts are closed, or at least only partially open, to him, while his is wide open to them. In 2 Corinthians 6:11—13, he insists that he is not withholding his affection for them and pleads with them to open their hearts also. Now Paul again tells them (7:3) that they have such a place in his heart that he would live or die with them. His love, like that of a father, includes (v. 4) great confidence and pride in them.

Paul has longed for news of their response to his earlier letter; his joy was "greater than ever" when Titus came with the good news of their sorrow and concern (vv. 5—7). But there is no mention of their love. In spite of their godly sorrow and the good results of the letter, Paul longs for what every Christian should be able to have from fellow Christians: love. As heat makes things expand, Chrysostom says, so the warmth of love will expand a man's heart. Christians often seem to have closed hearts—a coldness, a defense against love, and a Christian life that lacks the overflow of love towards others. To help such a person we may need to challenge such deceptions as the false tongues that had accused Paul of wrong, corruption, and exploitation (7:2). We may need to plead from the heart as he does. Whatever we do, we must work to help release the love that signifies the presence and power of Christ Jesus.

When sorrow is good. Sorrow can be terribly destructive, engendering bitterness, self-pity, and depression; causing despair, anger, and self-justification. We can see black as white and white as black in order to justify ourselves. Here Paul speaks of a different sort of sorrow (7:8—11), "godly sorrow." Paul says he is *happy* that the Corinthians have had such sorrow.

The difference between godly sorrow and ordinary sorrow lies in the result. "Godly sorrow brings repentance that leads to salvation and leaves no regret, but worldly sorrow brings death" (v. 10). The way back from sin is repentance, leading to God's forgiveness and cleansing. Instead of staying in the cloud we come out into the sunshine. Among the Corinthians the godly sorrow produced "earnestness, eagerness to clear themselves, indignation, alarm, longing, concern, and readiness to see justice done." Those explosive results show us so clearly what repentance is—not just saying "sorry" but incorporating a change of attitude, a different way of thinking, and an action to put things right wherever possible.

Paul's "painful" letter had the greater purpose, in God's intention, of producing such a result in the Corinthians—not just a correction of the wrongdoer or taking the side of the injured party. One of the surprises of Christian experience lies in seeing a higher purpose than the one close at hand, in circumstances and events. God may intend to stimulate faith in the face of deep testing, to lead to a new depth of prayer in facing the impossible, to establish a new standard of sacrificial giving in a single "faith" project. For the Corinthians, the result is a resurrection of the devotion they once had for Paul.

Repentance means action. David's psalm of repentance, Psalm 51, is a classic example of the good results of godly sorrow. An encouragement to believers down through the ages, it is a psalm to which many turn in times of failure or sin, a resource of spiritual help in experiences needing godly sorrow and repentance.

The early church took repentance seriously and often required outward evidence of genuine sorrow and of turning back to God. Bishop Ambrose required evidence of repentance by the Emperor Theodosius after he had massacred people as a reprisal. Ambrose forbade him Holy Communion for eight months and required the

Emperor to lie on the floor in sackcloth and promise that he would never carry out any further acts of capital punishment without thirty days' reconsideration. The Emperor submitted to this public penance.

When we are convicted of sin against the Lord and others, the quicker we turn to godly sorrow and repentance the better. Repentance is humbling (though seldom as much as it was for Emperor Theodosius!), but it is the immediate way back into fellowship with God and with our neighbor. The results of true repentance go further than merely making restitution; God uses it to his glory.

But—love. The Titus who returned to Paul was not just a reporter of what had happened but a Titus refreshed in his spirit. In spite of earlier problems, the Corinthians were still truly the Lord's and Paul was encouraged. Instead of receiving Titus with antagonism and resistance they had welcomed him "with fear and trembling" (v. 15). Titus's heart had opened to them, and he now held them in great affection.

In spite of all the good results from godly sorrow, however, there is no mention of the Corinthians' love for Paul. The Corinthians were slow learners in the school of Christ's love. While Paul can express "complete confidence" in them (v. 16), he cannot unconditionally rejoice in them, for they still withhold their affection from him. "If I do not have love, I am nothing," the apostle told them in his first letter; yet they have not yet learned the significance of that lesson of love.

Questions for Study and Discussion

1. How can Paul's exhortation to "come out and be separate" be distorted and used as justification for independence and pride? What does true separation mean?

2. How does the principle of being "equally yoked" relate to Proverbs 13:20—"He who walks with the wise grows wise, but a companion of fools suffers harm"? (NIV)

3. How can we live in the world and yet not partake of its standards (or lack of them)? What specific contrasts should be evident between the life of a Christian and the behavior of an unbeliever?

4. Compare Hebrews 12:11 with Paul's explanation of godly sorrow. What are the positive results of such sorrow?

CHAPTER 7

"GENEROUS" OR "STINGY"?

8:1—9:15

THE AMAZING DIVIDE BETWEEN GIVERS and non-givers is evident whenever I preach on giving. People will set their jaws, fold their arms, and determine not to be affected by the sermon! There is no steady upswing in the graph of Christian giving. People do not start to give and gradually get more generous and realistic in their giving; rather, some Christians are in the shallow water of giving and others are into it up to their necks. The plunge into the deep often comes suddenly: and only after a considerable battering on our defenses. We defend our "rights" to keep what we have, and even when we resolve to overhaul our giving, we often do not keep the resolution. But when we learn the secret of giving joyfully, we become committed to giving, and our money is released for the service of Christ.

Dragging feet

The reluctance to give is nothing new! The last place to get converted, when we come to Christ, is our wallet or handbag. Like many of us, the Corinthians were bad givers. They were full of themselves, confident that they were mature Christians, but Paul ruthlessly exposes them on the matter of giving. Chapters 8 and 9 offer the greatest challenge on giving in the whole of the Bible. If we will face up to that challenge seriously it will create a revolution in our giving. Paul's powerful argument is forceful and unanswerable, building point upon point to break through our defenses, leaving us with only one possible response.

Me first

First, Paul tackles the Corinthians' reluctance to give. Some Christians say, "If you do God's work in God's way, He will provide." But that is only part of the picture. It does not allow for human selfishness. As Malachi 3 demonstrates the blessing God wants to pour out is often held back because of the selfishness of his people. That selfishness needs to be challenged by preaching and teaching on giving.

But I'm not wealthy

Christians who believe themselves to be spiritually superior are often irritated by the example of those who more truly live for Christ. Paul pricks the Corinthians' self-satisfied consciences by lifting up before them the Macedonian churches, who had shown "rich generosity" (v. 2). The Corinthians, he implies, had the means to help but lacked an attitude of open-handedness; the rich generosity of the Macedonians, in contrast, arose out of extreme poverty.

Most people would reason that poverty provided a fair excuse not to give to others, but not so in Macedonia. Because their generosity was demonstrated in the midst of their own want, Paul can speak of their giving as "the grace that God has given" (v. 1), from the heart. "When I earn a salary then I'll start to give," says a student; but other Christian students have learned to give already. "If I earned more I would start giving," someone said to me; but the heart finds ways to give even in poverty, for it is not so much the amount but the attitude. The heart does not sit down to calculate, but responds in love when it sees a need. If, as many do, we start from "how little can I give," we remain trapped in self-centered attitudes. But the Macedonians started from "how much can I give" and probably surprised even themselves with the results!

Smiling as you give

"Well," says the Christian with a Corinthian attitude, "they must have found it very hard to give from their poverty." Not so, says Paul; although they were also in "severe trial," they gave out of "overflowing joy" (v. 2). The non-Christian or the unreleased Christian is staggered by such a statement, yet joy and giving are inseparably linked. Many congregations have taken on projects requiring considerable financial sacrifice; as the projects developed, the givers became more joyful and the non-givers or reluctant givers became more miserable. On the major Gift Days, a look across the congregation showed immediately who gave and who did not! One little old lady, living in a very simple house, wondered how she could give. Remembering the only valuable thing she possessed—a bone china dinner service stored away in a box—she sold it and brought the proceeds to my house. As she gave it to me her face was radiant and she was crying with joy. Jesus' words, "It is more blessed to give than to receive" (Acts 20:35) is a truth that flies in the face of the "get, get, get" world in which we live.

A tenth for God?

Paul speaks, in verse 3, of two standards of giving: "as much as they were able," and "beyond their ability." Generosity and reason move into the realm of daring and love. Elsewhere in Scripture we have the principle similarly expressed in terms of tithing (a tenth) and offering (e.g. in Malachi 3:8).

Tithes represent the proportionate side of giving. Christians who reject the idea of tithing on the grounds that it is Old Testament legalism need to check themselves that their New Testament freedom does not result in a lesser standard of giving! For many, the tithing of income is basic to Christian living. The usual reluctance must be overcome, but anyone who has adopted the tithing principle will acknowledge that it has opened a new dimension in their giving.

God has a first claim on our income, not the remnants of what we can afford when we have spent what we want on ourselves. We start by thinking of living on the other nine-tenths, putting the actual cash aside each week or month, setting up a separate bank account, or some other helpful method. The money for the Lord and for needs in the world is set aside, and regular giving is carefully planned. The sharing in the offering at church services becomes not an embarrassment but an act of worship.

Those who object to the idea of an actual tenth should think in terms of proportionate giving, lest giving remain static even when the income increases. When we begin to give proportionately, our giving corresponds to earnings or unemployment pay or pension or pocket money or whatever we receive. Ten dollars, a lot for some people, is minimal for others earning high salaries. When we complete our tax returns and see the total of our income for the past year, we can adjust our giving proportionately, so that the Lord and his work remain a priority both in our hearts and in our checkbooks.

Then start offering!

However, the tithing principle (whether before tax or after tax, whether after rent or mortgage payments or before) is only part of the story. The Macedonians gave proportionately ("as they were able") and beyond. The "beyond" is the realm of "offerings," often spontaneous, responding to special needs or as a special act of love towards the Lord. The woman with the alabaster box poured out her expensive ointment over Jesus. Although those watching regarded it as a waste, it was an act of love, and Jesus received it.

A young man in my youth group was deeply moved in his heart, and wanted to express his new love for God in an outward and visible way. He went to his bank, drew out his savings, and gave the money for the Lord's work. The next week I received a letter from his father protesting his son's action, demanding that the money be returned. But the young man did not want to have it returned. It was his special love gift, an offering of thanksgiving and love that had sprung from a renewed heart. Little wonder, perhaps, that the same young man later went on to offer his life for the Lord's service and is now in the ordained ministry.

Offerings may be collected on special Gift Days in our churches, when there is a special call for relief in a foreign country, for world need in general, for an urgent need in a friend's life. It may also be generated not by need but, as with the young man I mentioned, by overwhelming love or gratitude for the birth of a child, the healing of an illness, the answer to a special prayer, the loveliness of a holiday, the blessing of a sermon, a new understanding of God, the passing of exams, the love of a friend, or the memory of a life.

Often an envelope or a roll of bills appears in the offering plate or arrives through the mail with an anonymous note saying "in great gratitude to God for His blessing..." The offerings (v. 3), beyond the scale of proportionate giving, flowed because the Macedonians saw need and their hearts wanted to meet it. Little did they know that their loving act would be an example to Christians for thousands of years!

Please, may we give?

Not only did the Macedonians give generously, they "pleaded for the privilege" of sharing in this relief of others. Their attitude was diametrically opposed to the reluctance of those who try to look the other way when the offering is mentioned! They regarded giving not as a burden but as a privilege, an attitude that can only be attributed to the grace of God flowing in their hearts.

When we hear of need in another part of the world—the church undergoing persecution, or areas of famine and starvation, we should see the chance to help as a privilege. When we place our offering envelope in the Sunday collection, we should see it as a privilege. Ordinary Christians who learn to give with amazing sacrifice, can say "it was a privilege to be part of this investment for God."

And we give ourselves
Cash, however, can be an alternative to involvement; we must make sure that it is not so. The Macedonians (v. 5) did not allow their generosity to be "cold" but gave themselves first to the Lord and then to Paul, and to the concerns he shared with them. Giving to world need should be matched by a close interest in the facts of that need and of the people in need, an interest overflowing in prayer. When the need is close at hand we can often be personally involved in practical action.

In one parish where I worked there were some terrible houses, families living in appalling conditions. Because practical action was needed, people took time off from work and, as teams, tackled houses from top to bottom in cleaning, replacing beds and bedding, trying to restore homey-ness. Total transformations were achieved in a day because Christians gave themselves first, as well as money to buy the new furniture.

The Macedonians could not "come alongside" because of the distance, but they could share in love and, no doubt, prayer. Giving has to start with ourselves. If it not to be a remote "arm's length" activity, it has to spring out of a heart given to God and a life surrendered to Him.

A proof of love
Such an example must have embarrassed the Corinthians—possibly even stirred up resentment. But Paul continues to press his attack on their selfish defenses. Titus (v. 6) was being sent to collect this "act of grace" on their part. They would have to face him and not send

excuses from a distance. Paul urges them (with added encouragement in his commendation of their faith, knowledge, earnestness, and love for him) to "excel also in this grace of giving," the glaring deficiency in their Christian experience. They had to start giving as God intended. The reason is deeper than the money released; it is (v. 8) a test of "the sincerity of their love."

We easily say "I love God" and join in exuberant expressions of love and worship towards God as the Corinthians enjoyed doing. But if, in the realistic terms that affect our pocket and possessions, there is no love, the words we utter are empty and hollow.

The challenge to "think of the greatest amount you can give and then doubt it" which Bishop Alf Stanway commended wherever he went, presses us to action; yet that action can arise only out of love. Love and giving stimulate each other, so that the spiritual always outmatches the material; people who have learned to give from the heart in love are gloriously blessed in the process. Giving is a test of the genuineness of our love—a test which some Christians who exalt God in worship fail miserably.

Jesus the great giver

Love needs constant renewal, and there is no greater source of that renewal than our Lord Jesus. When our love grows weak, we are refreshed when we think of Him and of his sacrificial love for us on the Cross. Jesus Christ is our example, too, of giving, setting aside riches to become poor for us, that we might, through his poverty, become rich (v. 9). He gave all. He left everything. He gave himself utterly. We speak of being saved, having forgiveness, or gaining eternal life. But, in the context of the chapter, Paul speaks of our becoming rich.

"All things are yours," he said in 1 Corinthians 3:21, "and you are Christ's and Christ is God's" (RSV). How much is opened up to us, both now and in eternity, when we are "in Christ." All of it is only possible because Jesus gave to the uttermost. "Love so amazing, so divine, demands my life, my soul, my all."

Put your money where your mouth is

Apparently when Paul first asked the churches to give for this relief project, the Corinthians started doing so, but their enthusiasm or commitment did not go on to completion. Regrettably, such unfaithfulness is a frequent trait in church circles; the division between commitment and casualness is sharp. The committed person will carry through a task or responsibility with unswerving loyalty to Christ. The casual person will not have the same sense of commitment to the task because, it seems, he does not have the same commitment to Christ. He does not see that he is letting Christ down—only ("only"!) the church or other people. The task lapses. The promise to give fades away.

Paul challenges the Corinthians to return to the task and complete what "a year ago" they had promised. He assures them (v. 12) that they are not expected to give what they do not have (presumably they had offered that excuse) nor to give so that others are relieved while they are in difficulty (v. 13); rather, he is aiming at an equality that shares with those in need and receives from those who are in a better state of provision. This communal aspect of Christianity works out between churches, as part of the body of Christ.

The collectors are coming!

If the Corinthians had braced themselves for Titus coming to collect, they now had to brace themselves for a bigger shock: Titus will be accompanied by a brother who has been praised by all the churches for his service to the gospel, and another "zealous" brother who has "great confidence" in the Corinthians (8:16—9:5). They are being sent (9:5) to arrange to receive the "generous gift" the Corinthians had promised, and Paul suggests bringing Macedonians with him (v. 4). The Macedonian churches, set up as the example of giving, are sending representatives to spur the Corinthians to be like them! The "with me" of verse 4 slips in with the announcement regarding the Macedonians. Yes, Paul himself is coming!

Batter those defenses

Giving does not happen easily or readily; if a person is to become a giver, as God intends, then the brass gates of his defenses have to be shattered. It often takes a series of challenges, expositions, sermons, straight talking, and demonstrations of need, for the gates to fall. When they do fall, they fall forever, releasing an enormous amount of giving in time, money, and service for the kingdom of Christ. We have biblical warrant from this part of 2 Corinthians to hammer away about giving despite squeals of protest. Paul's goal is total surrender by the Corinthians on this issue and the release of love in giving.

Responsible distribution

Paul takes special care to be above criticism about this handling of money for God. 2 Corinthians 8:20—21 exhorts us to be acting rightly in the eyes of men as well as the eyes of God, taking great care in the counting and handling of offerings or any money given for the relief of need or the service of Christ. Money that is uncounted should never be handled alone; independent precautions should be taken. No one should be trusted to act on his own—for his sake and for the sake of the church.

In one church, a trusted member was discovered to have embezzled hundreds of dollars under the noses of other counters present at the table; the disclosure was extremely painful to everyone. More importantly, it dishonored Christ. When a speaker at a Christian meeting is given cash for travel, what check is there on the honesty of the treasurer? Even if he is strictly honest, he also needs to be *seen* to be honest "in the eyes of men" (8:21). Correct procedures are part of our responsibility for God.

Some Christian ministers and leaders do not heed this example from Scripture. Because they did not keep proper accounts, they could not answer the critics who wanted them "to give an account of their stewardship"; suspicion, pain, and strained fellowship resulted.

You reap what you sow
Paul applies the principle of sowing and reaping in the natural world to giving. He does not promise, of course, a straight sowing of cash and a harvest of cash as some persuasive cults imply: "Send forty dollars and within six months you will have ten times the amount back from God." Such statements are always accompanied by examples of Mr. X and Miss Y who are now rich because they gave to this guru, prophet or organization. Such promises are a despicable misapplication of the reaping pic-

ture in the Bible, putting the Christian faith into hard cash-investment terms, resulting in our own material benefit.

The New Testament does not rule out material blessings, but it does not speak in such materialistic terms as the give-and-get philosophy offers. Rather, the harvest is in richer spiritual terms. As thousands could testify, giving does bring spiritual blessing—as long as it is giving from the heart.

In Isaiah, chapter 1, God condemns the gifts brought to him because the people's hearts are so far from him. "One man gives freely," Proverbs 11:24 says, "yet grows all the richer; another withholds what he should give and only suffers want." Paul connects the act of giving with the attitude: God, he says in 9:7, loves a cheerful giver. He does not want gifts that are given out of a sense of duty or obligation or because the giver cannot avoid the persuasive techniques of the fund-raisers. He does not want reluctant giving but cheerful giving. On many Gift Days when we have had colossal targets for our giving I have said, on the basis of this text: "Don't give unless you do so in love for Christ . . . If you feel you ought to give but your heart is not in it, please do not give anything at all . . . we only want giving that springs from love for the Lord." Giving begins not in the checkbook, but in the heart.

Often fund-raising for Christian purposes is accomplished by the same means and methods as for a non-Christian cause: persuasion and manipulation. The leaders look for rich people to approach. Because giving comes from the heart, rich people often cannot give because they are too tied up with possessions, yet the ordinary person can give. God, who looks on the heart, tells us that only cheerful giving is acceptable. We can smile as we give, because we give in love!

God is no man's debtor

Although God does not *owe* us a material harvest, we are assured of God's provision for us when we give. The closed-fist philosophy brings little blessing, as Dickens' character Scrooge discovered. The open-handed approach means that God can meet us with his blessing; Malachi 3 promises blessings more than we can contain when we stop robbing God and bring the full tithes into the storehouse. He is able (v. 8) to make all grace abound towards us—the grace of giving in us is matched by fresh grace from him. We will have enough to meet our needs and will be enabled us to be more fruitful servants of his in the world. As Jesus' parable of the talents teaches, the reward of good service is further responsibility! Giving generously brings both physical and spiritual rewards: not only will we have an adequate store of seed (needs met) but a greater "harvest of righteousness."

The person who spends everything on himself—on records, books, films, entertainment, magazines, expensive vacations, luxuries—never finds satisfaction. He may find a fleeting enjoyment, but not the permanent satisfaction that grows deeper as the years go by. The giver finds that true satisfaction, and finds it deepening. Thus a sense of reward glowing within one's own spirit is part of the "harvest of righteousness" within us.

Another aspect of that harvest lies in recognizing the true value and priority of material things, having a true perspective on life. The "rich" in verse 11 refers to those rich in the spirit. We experience God's love and grace in Jesus; we respond in love and grace to others; God responds in more love and grace to us; we respond in further love and grace to others. In this increasing experience, the true giver becomes more and more a generous person sharing himself and his possessions with others.

The Corinthians are being encouraged to think in these God-intended terms. If they say "We can't afford to give to this relief fund" they ignore God's promised blessing and shrivel within their spirits. But if they say "We can't afford it, but we are going to share in any case," God enables them to give, and makes up what is given and more; then they will be able to give more, and know further blessing. People who have dared to give beyond any reasonable calculation have found God matching and supplying—a tax rebate, a gift, a raise in wages or salary—making up what has been given, often richly. The daring keep being surprised. The reluctant and stingy have no such surprises. Their giving (if it can be called that) has predictable results.

The by-product of thanksgiving

The by-product to real giving is thanksgiving (9:11—12). Paul envisions the recipients of the promised relief: fellow-believers in impoverished circumstances being materially helped and spiritually uplifted to thanksgiving. Refugee camps, beleaguered churches in countries ruled by atheistic governments, victims of drought or crop failure, hopeless thousands in war-torn lands—to these, Christians can extend love not only in prayer but in the basic material terms of cash.

In 1982 the Polish crisis motivated thousands of Christians to contribute for food and supplies for the churches to handle and distribute in that country. When the churches met and received the truck with its supplies for them, there would be joy and relief—but there would also be great thanksgiving to God for his mercy through his people. Those helped will praise God, says Paul (v. 13), not only because of the relief itself, but because it demonstrates the outworking of the gospel of Christ in the lives of the senders.

The social gospel and the Christian gospel are not rivals. The gospel of salvation in Jesus is the greatest need of the world, but the accompaniment of practical love and relief where it is needed should serve to glorify Christ and show the truth of the gospel.

Like the comfort of God, generous giving will have on-going effects; the recipients will give thanks to God and will pray for the givers. As they are drawn to the givers by the grace shown in the giving, new bonds of love will develop, accompanied by fresh blessing in answer to prayer. Fresh blessing will surely result in fresh action, and the cycle continues—giving and receiving blessings.

The inspiration of all giving, of course, is Jesus, the free gift of salvation offered to all who believe, the greatest gift offered to man. Our response must be one of exultant thanksgiving—in our life on earth, as we live and give and share, and then with the gathered company of God's people in heaven. Now, and then, we exclaim, "Thanks be to God for his indescribable gift!"

Questions for Study and Discussion

1. Discuss why giving is "more blessed" than receiving. Which is more difficult? How does giving release the Christian from self-centeredness?

2. Discuss the relationship between giving of one's material possessions and giving of oneself. How does a person's giving reflect his commitment to Jesus Christ?

3. The Scripture promises that we "reap what we sow." How is this principle demonstrated in both positive and negative results? Be specific.

4. What are some specific harvests that result from generous and cheerful giving?

CHAPTER 8

WAR AND CAPTIVITY

10:1—11:13

"DON'T YOU KNOW THERE'S A WAR ON?" The common remark during the Second World War, ought to be common among Christians. The sweetness and comfort that many Christians want is a far cry from the spiritual battleground revealed in Jesus' life and throughout the New Testament. "Our struggle is not against flesh and blood," says Paul in Ephesians 6, "but against the rulers, against authorities, against the powers of this dark world and against the spiritual forces of evil in the heavenly realms." Paul, in this part of 2 Corinthians, reveals to us the warfare being waged against the church, often from within. Satan aims to divert Christians from the truth in Jesus and to replace the true faith with false substitutes. The Corinthians had become easy prey to Satanic attack, and we, too, need to heed the warnings of this passage.

Into battle!

First, Paul calls us to prepare ourselves for battle, not just to defend against Satan, but to attack him. We are (v. 3) to "wage war," but not as the world does. Christianity cannot be forced on people at the point of a sword or gun or by offer of material aid. Such force has often been the tactic of heresies and, tragically, sometimes of the Christian church; but it has no place in God's plan. The church has to guard against the clever techniques or slick methodology of bringing the gospel to people with the persuasive methods of an encyclopedia salesman. If a person is forced into the kingdom by the church, the church will have to stand guard on him for all time; when the Holy Spirit draws someone, he will stand guard for eternity. "The weapons we fight with are not the weapons of the world." We are in a spiritual battle—a battle for the eternal destiny of men and women, a battle for the truth of God, a battle for the spiritual state of human beings.

This battle can only be won by spiritual weapons. Just as we cannot stop a bullet with a plastic raincoat, deflect a radio wave with a fly-swatter, or prevent germ warfare with a gun, so we cannot halt Satanic warfare with methods and gimmicks and organization. It can only be done by the word of God and prayer.

The one weapon effective enough to reach through to the inner man is the word—for the "word of God is living and active. Sharper than any double-edged sword, it penetrates even to dividing soul and spirit, joints and marrow; it judges the thoughts and attitudes of the heart" (Hebrews 4:12). All evangelism, witness, and contesting for the truth of God must concentrate on handling that sword effectively in communication and explanation and proclamation. At the same time, we need to be men and women who surround the work of witness with prayer.

So often prayer gatherings in churches are concerned merely with domestic and personal needs and do not begin to see the vital necessity of supporting the preaching, the evangelizing, and the outgoing work of the church with fervent prayer. We are waging war, and we are complete fools to think we can succeed by any other means than by the weapons of the word and prayer.

Watch their defenses crumble!

The spiritual weapons are powerful (vv. 4—5); they can demolish strongholds. As Christians we find ourselves in difficult situations—perhaps ridiculed in college by a professor who repeatedly uses us as a butt of his humor and tries to make us look ignorant simply because we are Christian. But the stronghold of that man's philosophy has no protection against spiritual weapons. Atheistic philosophies stand on a false foundation, and when they are really attacked they find their foundations crumbling.

Many Christians today have learned how to get inside the non-Christian philosophies to expose their weaknesses and press the holder of such a philosophy to the logical conclusions of his position. At the same time the effective witnesser is to show the eternal foundations of the faith in Christ.

During the first Festival of Light rally in London, when tens of thousands of Christians assembled to march to Hyde Park, many atheists went to the Park to vilify the Christians. One such man, a person of high intellect, went intending to attack the Christians. He was shaken by the force of the atheistic attack and the vile things being said; but he was more shaken by the love of the Christians in response. A crack appeared in his atheistic armor! Searching, he came to our church "by accident" during an evangelistic service. His defenses crumbled; he turned to Christ. Suddenly his intellect was geared to the new life he had found. He read several books a week and grew rapidly as a powerful advocate for Jesus. His stronghold—which had appeared so impregnable—had been destroyed by love and the word and prayer.

The deeply moving account of C. S. Lewis's conversion from atheism to Christ is a constant encouragement. As cracks in his atheistic position gradually appeared, he found himself exposed by the truth of God. He was, at first, a "most reluctant convert"! But his stronghold crumbled before the word of God. So let us take courage when we face people who seem impregnable in their stance against God. No one is impregnable against the word and prayer. We must pray for our enemies, for those who mock us and try to humiliate us intellectually, for the destroying of their strongholds; when opportunity arises, we must handle the sword of the word that it may break through every remaining defense!

Into captivity—for Christ

The goal is captivity to Christ (v. 5). At first, that seems to give credence to the false charge that we have to surrender intellectual integrity if we embrace Christianity. All who have come to Christ know that the opposite is true. The fear of the Lord really is the beginning of wisdom, and our whole way of thinking becomes transformed when we come to faith.

Such transformation is only possible because a person who surrenders to Jesus Christ as Savior and Lord receives the Holy Spirit. The Holy Spirit searches and knows the things of God and shows them to us (1 Cor. 2). We begin to see, as never before, how utterly relevant God's truth is to the world in which we live—God's analysis of man, God's way of living, God's way for human beings to be made right with him, God's values of life and justice. This is *God's* world; everything fits into that frame and makes sense. We are created in the image of God—a little lower than the angels, not just a little higher than the animals. The totality of our thinking changes.

When Paul speaks of bringing every thought into captivity—into obedience to Christ—he is speaking of freedom in place of the captivity and bondage in which man stands before he turns to Christ, of being in Christ who is the way, the truth and the life.

Under authority

The New Testament always presents a double picture: the victory of Christ in which we share eternally when we turn to him, and the "mopping up" operations that go on for life. We are dead in Christ and alive in Christ—that is our eternal state. But much needs to be "put off" and "put on" as Ephesians 4 and Colossians 3 spell out frankly. It is not, as some teach, that because we are dead and risen we have nothing more to do about practical holiness. Rather, *because* we are dead and risen, we should live out what we are. We should wage war on the tangles of sin and the infection of evil, fostering all that belongs to the Spirit of God in love, fruitfulness and goodness. Paul pleads in verses 5 and 6 for the Corinthians to get on with submission to the truth of God and to stop disobeying what God has revealed to them in Christ.

The Corinthians advocated a happy, effervescent worship gathering, but ignored a close attention to the word of God and to living in obedience to the revealed truth of God. Paul's responsibility is to exercise discipline and to "punish disobedience." He cannot tolerate a free-for-all, with "every man doing what he thinks is right"; there must be a growing concern to live as Christ wants us to live. Paul's discipline is not authoritarian—the leader telling people what to do and what not to do, like the discipling-legalism that is particularly common in some groups of Christians today—but authority of and submission to the word. The leader or teacher only has authority as he handles the authoritative word and leads in the light of it.

Many Christians resent correction. A gentle exposure of a fault, a bad temper, a lack of love, a hypercritical approach causes the exposed person to resent it and leave the church. Criticism or correction of our lives must be brought to the bar of Scripture and, where that correction is valid, we must repent and submit ourselves afresh to the glad captivity of Christ! Those who resisted Paul and rejected what he was saying would have to face discipline by him; they could not go off to another church in Corinth!

Beyond comparison?

Smug self-confidence can be the most difficult barrier of all to Christian reality. When a Christian meets an atheist or an agnostic both sides know clearly where they stand. But the person who thinks he is all right and a perfectly good Christian ("better than some who go to church") has to be shown what he is really like before God. Verses 7—18 refer to such people, those who only look "on the surface of things." The smooth-speaking and attractive false apostles in Corinth had mesmerized the church. They were not a bit like Paul, whose appearance was apparently not very attractive. The Corinthians had committed themselves to those false apostles, believing that they were right and Paul was wrong, almost doubting that Paul was a genuine Christian. He had not "arrived" like them—he was still not at their higher spiritual level.

Paul responds, in effect, (v. 7) "At least regard us as fellow-Christians!" Then he deftly begins to expose their thinking (v. 12ff). They are comparing themselves with themselves! They look at the false apostles in their midst and are content if they have the same level of Christian living—possibly the same "badges" of particular gifts or actions or ways in worship, depending on built-in security which Paul seeks to destroy. The Corinthians were captive not to the obedience of Christ but to the obedience of men. There is only one possible valid comparison—and that is measuring ourselves by Christ Jesus himself.

Who is Lord?

Paul had every justification to write strongly to the Corinthians. He was their spiritual father. They were part of the harvest field assigned to him by the Lord. As a spiritual father to them he has a continuing concern and care. He wants to see his "children in the faith" growing, and verse 15 suggests that the Corinthians were trying to hinder his activity and influence among them. Paul does not let go easily, but at the same time, he does not want to be so caught up sorting out the Corinthians that he is

prevented from "preaching the gospel in regions beyond" (v. 16). Paul has the burning heart of an evangelist,
looking outward for opportunities to exercise that
mission.

Although Paul could justifiably boast about his mission
to Corinth, he turns the argument back to its true perspective: if we are going to boast at all, let us "boast in the
Lord." If we want commendation, let us not seek it by
self-congratulation and smug self-satisfaction, but rather
at the feet of Christ. Paul presses the point: if we do not
bring every thought into obedience to Christ, we cannot
expect Christ's commendation. Christ must always be at
the center, and everything we do must be brought to his
feet. In everything—everything—Christ must be pre-
eminent.

The third party
The letter now becomes even more serious. The warfare
waged by Satan has had shattering effects upon the
Corinthians. Those who uphold the Corinthian church
as the model for Christian worship and church life never
seem to realize that Corinth went into heresy. When experience matters most, truth suffers.

Biblical truth and spiritual experience go hand in hand
and must never be divorced. Truth without experience
is deadly; experience without truth is disastrous. Corinth
is an example of such disaster. 2 Corinthians 11:1—5,
presents a "church's health warning." The passion of
Paul's heart bursts out in anguish. The church is the
bride of Christ; Paul, in Ephesians 5, explains that the
Lord Jesus longs for the bride to be without spot, or
wrinkle or any blemish. He had brought them to Christ,
like the friend of the bridegroom, and he wanted them to
have eyes for Jesus only. This is Paul's own longing—to

be found in Christ, to grow in Christ, to be more like
Christ. Now he had to look on while a "third party" diverted the Corinthians from Christ. Paul has no doubt
about the source and motivation of these false apostles—
it is Satan, whose tactics always divert Christians from the
Lord, as he did Eve.

Satan in at the top

Verses 13—15 present the devastating description of
those false apostles. To the Corinthians, who believed
that these men were messengers of God and super-
spiritual apostles, Paul's words pierced deep: "Such men
are false apostles, deceitful workmen, masquerading as
apostles of Christ." Howls of opposition would arise if we
tendered such accusations today, for we have often been
soft towards heresy and so let it flourish. But Paul presses
the point harder still. These apostles are not just false—
they are Satanic. They are Satan's servants masquerading
as servants of righteousness. What better tactic can an
enemy have than to infiltrate the very ranks and leadership of his enemy, even to take command? If Satan could
infiltrate the leadership of the Christian church at local
or national or international level, would he not do it? Has
he not done it? A witch hunt is not necessary, for the test
is obedience to Christ and his word. Leadership that
swerves from obedience is either on the slippery slope to
error or has already been infiltrated by the enemy. We
must never think that we can test by any test except
Christ, whatever the "rank" of the Christian leader.

Turned from Christ

The Corinthians (vv. 3—6) had been diverted from their
"sincere and pure devotion to Christ" by persuasive
preachers. The untrained speaking of Paul (v. 6) seemed

far inferior to those smooth-tongued "super-apostles" (v. 5). Yet it is content that matters, not eloquence or oratory. Is it true? Is it in accordance with God's word? Does it glorify Jesus? "I may not be a trained speaker," Paul says (v. 6), "but I do have knowledge." Because the Corinthians could not discern the importance of that knowledge, they fell into three major heretical errors.

Another Jesus

The first error was to turn to "another Jesus." The Greek word means a "different kind" of Jesus, not a different Jesus, perhaps denying the divinity of Christ, perhaps de-emphasizing his humanity. Throughout the history of Christianity, and into the present day, some try to present Jesus as man only—a good man, a teacher, an example, but not God. Some say he was not born of the Holy Spirit, others that he had no existence prior to his birth by Mary. Some speak of Jesus as the human man and Christ as the divine idea; others deny the divinity of Jesus and say that only a likeness died on the Cross; yet others so minimize the human side of Jesus, the reality of his earthly life and death seems not to matter as long as we have a mystical experience of his resurrection life today. The simplicity and clarity of the true Jesus Christ is revealed to us in the New Testament—he is truly God and truly man. That sincere and pure devotion to Christ is central to a living Christian faith; we must test the theories of theologians by the one test God has given us —Scripture.

A different spirit

The second error was to receive "a different spirit." The Greek means a different spirit altogether, not a different kind of spirit. These Christians in Corinth, so proud of their spiritual experiences, were in fact not indwelt by the Holy Spirit, but were exhibiting a pseudo-spirituality.

John sustains a similar charge in his first letter, (4:1—3). "Test the spirits," he says. "This is how you can recognize the spirit of God: Every spirit that acknowledges that Jesus Christ has come in the flesh is from God, but every spirit that does not acknowledge Jesus is not from God." Then he declares: "This is the spirit of antichrist." Was the apparent spirituality in Corinth actually a spirit of antichrist, rotting away spiritual foundations from within? The New Testament interprets the concept of a completely different spirit in no other way. If it is not the Holy Spirit it must be the counterfeit and deceiving spirit of antichrist.

The New Testament also encourages us to look for the fruit of a person's life as the test. Jesus, in his Sermon on the Mount, (Matt. 7:15—23) tells us to test all prophets by their fruit: "By their fruit you will recognize them." Some would put their trust in special works, in prophesying, driving out demons, and performing miracles. Like some today, they no doubt regarded these as marks of special spiritual grace. When they come to Jesus, calling him Lord, and bringing evidence of their works, he will reply, "I never knew you." Prophesying and miracles are not wrong, but they are not a means of assurance. Fruit—love, joy, peace, holiness of life—is God's test.

Because such fruit seemed to have little place in the Corinthian thinking, Paul has to major on the importance and priority of love (1 Corinthians 13) in the middle of his chapters on gifts. The true Spirit of God will bring forth his fruit, the character of Jesus, in the believer. The counterfeit spirit, the Antichrist, will be evidenced by "pushiness," self-concern, spiritual pride and superiority, over-attention to the occult and spirit-activities, and carelessness with the truth.

A *different gospel*

The third error was the Corinthians' acceptance of a "different gospel." Again, the Greek means a different gospel altogether, not a different version of the gospel. Galatians 1:6—9 offers a blistering attack on the acceptance of "another gospel" which, says Paul, is "no gospel at all." He continues in those searing words: "Even if we or an angel from heaven should preach a gospel other than the one we preached to you, let him be eternally condemned!" Paul does not even hint at the idea, prevalent even today, that salvation can be by other means than the grace of God in Jesus Christ and his sacrifice for our sins on the Cross. Justification is by faith through grace; salvation is a gift from God, never to be earned. Often, the alternative offered seems more attractive, easier to accept, less demanding, more inclusive, and so, like the Corinthians, many turn to it "easily enough" (v. 4). But anything that subtracts from this gospel or adds to it is not the gospel at all.

In the center of the ring

Paul loves the Corinthians deeply in spite of their foolishness. For the false teachers, he knows, "their end will be what their actions deserve" (v. 15). But he does not want the end of these his "children in the faith" in Corinth to be the same. He wages, therefore, an all-out rescue operation to restore them to sincere and pure devotion to Christ. We are in a spiritual war; a quiet retreat is not an option for a Christian. Our aim, like Paul's, must always be to "take captive every thought to make it obedient to Christ."

Questions for Study and Discussion

1. What kind of warfare are we as Christians engaged in? List some of the specific enemies we encounter in the battle.

2. How does "bringing every thought into captivity to Christ" relate to the centrality of Christ described in Colossians 1? Specifically, how do we submit all things to the Lordship of Christ?

3. The Corinthians found a number of excuses to rationalize their rebellion against Paul's correction of them. What excuses do Christians in the present day offer when they desire to resist correction? What should be our attitude toward exposure and correction of our faults?

4. In what ways do modern Christians turn to "another Jesus"?

CHAPTER 9

POWER, GRACE, AND TESTING

11:16—13:14

THE VALUE AND PURPOSE OF SUFFERING was not taught by the "superlative apostles"; the Corinthian leaders, rather, measured "superiority" in terms of eloquent speaking and freedom from trouble. Paul, however, believes that the power of God has been manifested in his life despite his lack of natural eloquence; in the sufferings, hardships, and persecutions of his Christian service, the power of God had unmistakably triumphed. Power was shown in weakness—and what power!

Loss of discernment

Goaded by the undiscerning naiveté of the Corinthian leaders, Paul "boasts" of himself (11:17), not because such boasting is normal, but because it is his only possible response to them.

When Christians digress from the centrality of Christ, they seem to lose discernment. The Corinthians thought themselves wise (v. 19), yet submitted to being enslaved, exploited, and taken advantage of. Even today, heretical movements centered in one person produce terrible results such as the Jonestown massacre in Guyana. People in such groups surrender goods, houses, and money; they put themselves totally under the control of the leader. Other diversions from the centrality of Jesus may not turn to heresy, but have the same characteristics that Paul discerns among the Corinthians.

Ready for anything

Paul boasts, then, of the same Jewish ancestry as the false apostles; he is equally a servant of Christ, but there the comparison ceases. Instead of enjoying a comfortable, self-indulgent, egocentric Christianity, he reached the world of his day with courage and daring and vision that still leaves us breathless after 2,000 years. What Paul achieved for Christ in the days of slow travel and poor communication is staggering, but it was achieved at great cost—imprisonment, flogging, exposure, thirty-nine lashes (five times), beating, stoning, shipwreck, and all sorts of dangers on the land. The Jews hated him; the Gentiles hated him. False believers also presented danger; he always had to exercise discernment, to judge not by outward appearances or commendations. Loss of sleep, long hours of work, hunger, thirst, cold—all had been in his experience. And in addition, he faced "daily the pressure of my concern for all the churches."

The sufferings Paul endured would never have occurred if he had not been in the glad service of his Master. He would have been safe back in his Jewish enclave, teaching the law, not escaping over a city wall in a basket (v. 33)! Paul urges the Corinthians not to despise his experiences, clinging to their false ideas of victorious

Christianity. This list is his track record of committed service for his Lord, not to earn salvation, but to live out his membership in the body of Christ and his call as a true apostle for Jesus Christ.

Take up the cross

Paul's record of committed missionary service has been an inspiration and challenge to Christians ever since, and much could be added to Paul's list in the record of Christian service for the past two thousand years. With amazing courage early witnesses and missionaries pioneered into deadly areas of the world, extending the long and honorable roll of martyrs for the gospel of Jesus. Like them, we are not to "play it safe" but to take up the cross and to follow Christ whatever the cost.

Experience of glory

The false apostles had apparently told thrilling accounts of their special visions and direct communication from God. "God has told me" is a statement that neither invites nor allows disagreement! Many Christians today fail to use any discernment but submit meekly to what they feel must be very spiritual indeed.

Paul's emphasis on truth and Christian living was regarded as somewhat inferior in comparison. If the Corinthians want to think in those terms, Paul can share his own seventh-heaven experience. Clearly the "man in Christ" in verse 2 of chapter 12 is himself. It was obviously a deep and overwhelming experience that carried him beyond himself—a manifestation of the power and love of God—almost a transfiguration experience.

Those times when the Lord overwhelms us with a taste of glory, with his presence and love, are wonderful times. But they are not the bread and butter of Christian experience. They are the special tokens of love as a fore-taste of heaven. The false apostles may boast in those terms but they are wrong to do so, says Paul: "I will not boast . . . except about my weaknesses." We may rejoice and wonder at the glory experiences of Jesus in his Transfiguration, yet we know that the greater glory of Jesus was in his Cross. In the darkness of Calvary, under the darkened sky, hearing the bereft soul crying "My God, my God," we see the glory; earlier, in the Garden of Gethsemane where sweat fell as drops of blood, we see the glory; before that, as Jesus touches the leper and loves the sinner, we see the glory. When John writes, "Now is the Son of Man glorified and God is glorified in him," he refers to the cross and the atonement (John 13:31). Although we may have special tastes of glory to come, the pathway for the followers of Jesus usually means glory through suffering.

Healing for all?

There are many today who deny the place of suffering in the Christian's life, who sincerely believe that if the kingdom came with Jesus it must mean wholeness of body as well as of soul. Such people sometimes bring healing and comfort, but they also leave a trail of despondent wrecks along the way. Their teaching denies that verses 7—10 have anything to do with physical suffering. But these verses teach us a theology of healing and a theology of suffering—for the truth of the Bible is not "either/or" but "both/and."

A theology of healing

First, Paul sets forth the theology of healing. "Three times I pleaded with the Lord to take it away," Paul writes

of his "thorn in the flesh" (v. 7). Those who want to deny
that this is a physical affliction suggest it was some sin in
his life; but sin would demand repentance. "Flesh" is
flesh, the physical body, and the thorn suggests something that happened to Paul rather than something he
brought on himself—perhaps, some scholars believe, his
failing eyesight.

Paul commits the problem to the Lord in deliberate
prayer. "Three times" he sets aside special times of
prayer, perhaps separated by weeks rather than days. He
may have called together his friends to pray or asked
others to lay on hands. Healing prayer too easily becomes
just another item on a prayer list; Paul indicates that it
needs special treatment by Christians: a group coming
together for an evening of prayer and laying on of
hands, or a special gathering of close Christian friends.

Often during those prayer times or as a result of them
there is deliverance or healing, and we are overjoyed at
the result of prayer to our loving Father. In other cases,
the conviction gradually grows that healing is not the
pathway of God's glory for the person we are praying
for. To persist even to the day of death, as some have
done, is to lose the glory of Christ. Instead, we test the
conviction before God, and begin to alter our prayer as
Paul did. Beyond putting up with sufferings, he goes on
to boast in them (v. 9) and delight in them! Along with
his theology of healing, Paul demonstrates a theology of
suffering—that it can be a means of glory to Christ.

But didn't Christ "carry our sicknesses"?

Because Matthew 8:17 says that Christ has carried our
sicknesses, the Christian may believe that on the cross
Christ died for our sins and our sicknesses thus bringing

wholeness to the believer. But the word for sicknesses in Matthew 8:17 is *asthenia;* in 2 Cor. 12:9 the word translated "weaknesses" is *asthenia;* and the word translated "weaknesses" in verse 10 is also *asthenia.* If wholeness were the Christian's right, Paul could hardly rejoice in his weaknesses.

If an illness persists and we are not healed; if we have prayed deliberately on several occasions and have begun to sense the Spirit's response that, instead, this is to be a pathway of suffering, then we can begin to glory in our weakness—for Christ's sake.

The exemplary Christians we have ever known, in most cases, are those who have triumphed in the midst of suffering, who, like quadriplegic artist Joni Eareckson Tada, have lived a life more abundant even though they are disabled or suffer.

Grace and glory

If such a triumphing in our weaknesses was by our own strength, by our resolve to glorify Jesus, that would be good in itself; but we do not have to do it alone. The glorious truth is the Lord's personal assurance to Paul: "My grace is sufficient for you, for my power is made perfect in weakness." Once we accept his pathway we will begin to know depths of grace we never knew before and find a strength that is not our own.

An elderly Salvation Army officer with whom I stayed during a mission at a local church was wracked with asthma and confined to his bed. Yet, the moment we returned from the meetings he wanted to know what had happened, for he had been praying with all his heart. He was thrilled with reports of blessing and concerned with reports of opposition or problem. His face radiated the glow of Jesus, the presence of the Lord filled that bedroom as we shared with that dear man who turned illness into glory.

Triumph and power

Paul is able to turn his thorn into triumph; he is able to take (v. 10) insults, hardships, persecutions, difficulties, and so to learn a whole new dimension of Christian living: "when I am weak, then I am strong."

Strength comes when we are thrown back upon the grace and strength of the Lord Jesus. When we are fit and well, we are tempted to rely on our own strength. The words "But he said" (v. 9) are indicative of an ongoing strength; "said" is in the perfect tense—that the experience is an ongoing comfort to Paul's soul—and "sufficient" can also mean "satisfied." God is not promising just enough grace to get us through, but a deeper balm to our soul that springs from knowing God is in this experience and we are in His will.

Paul's desire is to know the power of Christ and to glorify Christ, not in deliverance from suffering but in suffering itself. If we only think of power in terms of deliverance we may miss the blessing and glory God intends in our lives.

Fruit is always the test

Paul's final attack against the false apostles relates to the emphasis on signs rather than fruit, on "miracle power" rather than "endurance power."

Signs, wonders and miracles had been done among them by Paul. The Corinthians had become so caught up with that sort of evidence that they seemed to have lost sight of the fruit of the Spirit. Paul fears (v. 20) that there may be quarreling, jealousy, outbursts of anger, factions, slander, gossip, arrogance, and disorder amongst them; as well, he fears finding those earlier condemned for impurity, sexual sin, and debauchery still around in the church, still not having repented of their sin.

"Super-spiritual" experience diverts us from living in obedience to Christ. At a retreat years ago, we met a resident director who regarded himself as far superior spiritually to all the rest of us. He pressed his apparently exuberant experience on us, but before the houseparty ended he was caught stealing and later was shown to be an adulterer. Fruit is always the test; Paul is looking for fruit, teaching on it, and disciplining over it. The love and concern he has as a father to his children (v. 14) will not weaken his reproof of sin and his action against those who had gone on sinning in spite of his earlier warnings (13:1—2).

Paul exercises caution that a charge will have to be supported by the testimony of two or three witnesses, as Jesus commands in Matthew 18:16. If leaders react and form a judgment on the testimony of one person, or on a rumor, they may find themselves acting unjustly. But if anybody in Corinth hoped that Paul, in his physical weakness, would also show weakness in his dealing with them, they were mistaken.

Paul spells out the weakness-power combination in a slightly different way in 13:3—4. Christ, crucified in weakness, is now the Lord of power and authority. Similarly, we are both weak in Christ and strong in Christ to serve him and the church. Power is linked to the inner and spiritual rather than to the outward and physical.

Time for examination

Paul's letter demands a response. Paul is not able to be there at the moment the letter is read, even though he hopes to go to Corinth before long. So he puts the burden of response on his hearers. They are to examine themselves (13:5)—not in morbid introspection, but in sober self-examination of how they stand before Christ.

Introspection is an end in itself, but self-examination is a means to an end. The basic test is that "Christ is in us." The Corinthians might consider Paul a failure, but Paul gently says that even if they think that, it is no excuse for them not to desire to live as the Lord intends. His prayer (v. 9) is for their perfection or "improvement" (RSV). Despite the Corinthians' spiritual pride, Paul knows they have a long way to go and he prays that they may go forward and not stay in their present self-satisfied state. When he comes to them (v. 10) he intends to build them up, for maturity in Christ is Paul's heart's desire for every Christian.

And so—farewell

Paul's final greeting encourages the Corinthians to aim at perfection or completeness. The loss of that ambition in a Christian can only result in a stagnant Christian faith. Paul urges them to listen to his appeal; the expressions of love and peace, the urging to greet one another with a holy kiss (or a good handshake or a great hug), encourage them to demonstrate the openness of peace and love that should mark the life of a church family anywhere.

The Closing

The last verse of 2 Corinthians is familiar to us as a bene-diction. Perhaps we hear it so often that we do not ponder what is being prayed for one another. "The grace of our Lord Jesus Christ" echoes that sentence in chapter 8 "you know the grace of our Lord Jesus Christ . . . though he was rich, he became poor." We bask in the wonder of Christ's love and grace. The "love of God" assures us afresh that nothing in all creation can separate us from that love. The "fellowship of the Holy Spirit" is one of the constant privileges of being in Christ, a bond that stretches across time and space, that unites us to millions we have never met, and that enables us to see barriers broken down in the local fellowship of believers. The entire expression embraces the totality of life in Christ as part of the family of God: "May the grace of the Lord Jesus Christ, and the love of God, and the fellowship of the Holy Spirit be with you all."

Questions for Study and Discussion

1. How can we reconcile the seeming contradiction between God's promise to heal and the persistence of suffering and disease?

2. Discuss specific instances in which God's grace has been sufficient for weaknesses in your own life.

3. Jesus said, "By their fruits you shall know them." What kind of fruit is developed through suffering?

4. In what specific ways can we examine ourselves to evaluate our standing before Christ? What are some false standards of measurement used to evaluate spiritual growth? What are the biblical standards?

More Books to Ignite Your Faith

Breaking the Prayer Barrier by Michael Baughen. A readable and practical book that tells how to break the prayer barrier and get through to God.

Bursting the Wineskins by Michael Cassidy. An autobiography that describes a burgeoning movement of the Holy Spirit and demonstrates God's radical power in changed human lives.

Called & Committed: World-Changing Discipleship by David Watson. Challenges us to demonstrate unreserved commitment to Christ, to become the kind of disciples who can change the world.

Finders Keepers by Dee Brestin. Shows how evangelism and discipleship can be natural outgrowths of developing genuine friendships with non-Christians; offers practical insights on personal and small-group evangelism.

Flirting with the World by John White. Exposes undeniable proof that most Christians are not only *in* but *of* the world and calls us to radical repentance, true fellowship, and serious study of God's Word.

George Müller: Delighted in God by Roger Steer. Shows how a man's total faith in God resulted in miraculous provision and answers to prayer.

Grow & Flourish by David Watson. Daily devotional readings for an entire year offer powerful, biblical insights and motivation for change and growth.

The Moses Principle: Leadership & the Venture of Faith by Michael Baughen. Studies in the life of Moses, combined with the author's experiences, reveal principles of faith in God that can help us accomplish the humanly impossible.

You Are My God by David Watson. "Personal, honest, winsome, instructive, and inspiring. All who are open to the power of the Word and the Spirit will be enriched by this record of his pilgrimage"—David A. Hubbard.

Available from your favorite bookstore, or from **Harold Shaw Publishers,** Box 567, Wheaton, Illinois 60189.